THE IRISH CIVIL WAR

THE IRISH
CIVIL WAR

An Illustrated History

Helen Litton

Picture Research by Peter Costello

WOLFHOUND PRESS

Reprinted 1997
First published 1995 by
WOLFHOUND PRESS Ltd
68 Mountjoy Square
Dublin 1

British Library Cataloguing in Publication Data
A catalogue record for this book is available from the British Library

ISBN 086327 480 3

The publishers have made every reasonable effort to contact the copyright
holders of material reproduced in this book. If any involuntary infringement
of copyright has occurred, sincere apologies are offered and the owners of
such copyright are requested to contact the publishers.

10 9 8 7 6 5 4 3 2

Cover design: Slick Fish Design, Dublin
Cover painting: *An Allegory*, Seán Keating. Courtesy of The National Gallery
Typesetting: Wolfhound Press

CONTENTS

THE NIGHT THE TREATY WAS SIGNED

An interesting fact about this huge canvas is that it was painted almost entirely from living models, many of whom participated in the original Gold Rush.

The third from the right in the extreme top corner is now a principal officer in the Department of F——-ce on a salary of £815 to £915 a year, exclusive of bonus. Though badly placed at the Macroom bend, he gained ground rapidly on the Straight Tipperary stretch and drawing into the lead passing thro' Naas was never afterwards headed.

Mr. Eustace O'Honovan, who occupies third place in the picture, dropped back to almost last soon after passing Monasterevan and the best he could do was a clerical officership in the Department of Posts and Telegraphs.

Mr. Herbert O'Twomey, who is seen in the lead in the picture, kept up a rare bat all the way till coming into Lucan, when his wooden leg and the wind resistance to his nightgown began to tell against him. However, he finished a creditable sixth and secured a Junior Administrative post shortly after the abolition of the Entrance Examination for the position.

The gentleman who is seen in the picture taking the short cut over the wall and across the fields, ran into second place passing Sallins, but failed to overhaul the leader. He secured a £900 to £975 position in the Land Commission, and five hours after his appointment, sent home for his brother, only to find that the latter had secured a seat up on a lorry and had already established himself in the Office of Public Works.

Nothing definite is known of the official history of the Mr. M. O'Keeffe who is seen extricating himself from an awkward position on the left of the picture, but a friend of ours who addressed an appeal recently to the Revenue Department is of opinion that the reply he got was from him.

(from *Dublin Opinion*)

INTRODUCTION

I approached this project in a fog of relative ignorance about the Irish Civil War and the events surrounding it, because I am part of the generations of schoolchildren which were only taught Irish history up to, at best, 1921. The Irish Free State may as well not have existed at all.

As I researched for the book, I came to feel that we had been short-changed to some extent, ignorant of the foundations of the state in which we were citizens. We were equally uninformed about the foundation of the Northern Ireland state, and I was surprised to learn how closely events in both parts of Ireland were linked at this time.

I have done my best to write a clear, straightforward narrative, outlining the main events, and the circumstances that drove people to act as they did, but it was a very difficult job. Newspaper quotes, personal reminiscences and contemporary photographs and illustrations are chosen to try to provide an atmosphere of the times. Biographical notes on the main characters mentioned are on pp146–149.

The book was written for people who are interested in the confusing sequence of events by which the south of Ireland moved from being a colonial possession, to a Free State, and ultimately to a Republic. It is impossible that some readers will not be offended by imagining a leaning to one side or the other, but I am not emotionally involved in this story, on either side.

I particularly wish to thank Peter Costello, who willingly deployed his unparalleled experience in picture research and compilation. I am in debt to the resources of the National Library of Ireland, the Royal Society of Antiquaries of Ireland and the Archives Department, University College Dublin. I must also thank Wolfhound Press for their support and efficiency, and for giving me the opportunity to produce this book.

CHAPTER I

Genesis

The Irish Civil War arose, essentially, from the signing of a Treaty with Britain, and the subsequent quarrel about the meaning of this Treaty – what was gained or lost. Was it what the revolutionaries of 1798, 1867, 1916 had died for? Was it a first step away from the devastated past and the log-jammed present, towards what might ultimately end in a free Ireland?

Long debates were held in Dáil Eireann (the parliament) on whether to accept the Treaty or not. Reading them now, the words leap off the page, burning with anger, passion and conviction, and the language is apocalyptic. No middle way was possible; the Treaty was either something Robert Emmet or Wolfe Tone might have welcomed, a step towards complete freedom, or it was a cowardly betrayal of Ireland's martyrs, particularly the most recent.

Some of the flavour emerges in a letter written by Kathleen Clarke, in a script barely legible with rage: 'Great God did I ever think I'd live to see it, to see men who were the bravest, now fooled and blinded by a juggle of words into the belief that this Treaty means a realization of our highest ideals...' In a forceful contribution to the debate, she stated: 'I heard big strong military men say here they would vote for this Treaty which necessarily means taking an Oath of

Allegiance, and I tell those men there is not enough power to force me, nor eloquence to influence me in the whole British Empire into taking that Oath, though I am only a frail scrap of humanity'.

Indeed, the women members were among the fiercest in the Dáil debates, passionately proclaiming their right to speak for the husbands, sons and brothers who had died in 1916. Mary MacSwiney insisted:

'You men that talk need not talk to us about war. It is the women who suffer...You can go out in the excitement of the fight and it brings its own honour and its own glory. We have to sit at home and work in more humble ways, we have to endure the agony, ... the torture of misery and the privations which war brings, the horror of nightly visitations to our houses and their consequences. It is easier for you than it is for us, but you will not find in Ireland a woman who has suffered who today will talk as the soldiers here today have talked... If [England] exterminates the men, the women will take their places, and if she exterminates the women, the children are rising fast...'

Despite all this fevered eloquence, the fact remained that the vast majority of the people of Ireland were willing to accept the Treaty, whether they believed it was the best Ireland would ever get, or whether they were 'stepping-stoners', hoping that it would lead to better things. The country had suffered war, atrocities and reprisals for years, and violence and fear had exhausted the population. This was later expressed contemptuously by Máire Comerford: '...it seemed a lot easier to tell a few lies and take a few oaths and go into the British Commonwealth than to continue with the fight'. But it was not as simple as that.

Background To The Treaty

After the Easter Rising of 1916, which proclaimed a Republic of Ireland, the Irish Volunteers were reorganised, and gradually became known as the Irish Republican Army (IRA). Sinn Féin, under its leaders Arthur Griffith and Eamon de Valera, asserted control over this army, but in reality it was still commanded by the secret Irish Republican Brotherhood, which had masterminded the 1916 Rising, and was now headed by Michael Collins.

In the general election of December 1918, Sinn Féin won 73 of the 105 seats contested, but refused to attend the House of Commons in Westminster. Instead they established the first Dáil Eireann (parliament of the Republic), which could rarely meet because many of its members were in prison or on the run. In 1919 Sinn Féin, and Dáil Eireann, were banned by the British authorities. Meanwhile a guerrilla war, beginning on a small scale, gradually escalated. The official start of this War of Independence is dated to an ambush at Solo-headbeg, Co. Tipperary, on 21 January 1919, when the 3rd Tipperary Brigade of the IRA ambushed members of the Royal Irish Constabulary, killing two. As this war progressed, the IRA made more and more of the decisions, marginalising the Sinn Féin politicians.

The War of Independence was mainly limited to Dublin and the province of Munster, and IRA victories were few and far between. They were short of arms and supplies, communications were extremely difficult, and many of the fighters were untrained youths. Conflict consisted largely of ambushes by Republican 'flying columns', and these were followed by brutal reprisals, usually inflicted on the local civilian population. British defence was strengthened by the 'Black and Tans' and the 'Auxiliaries', auxiliary police forces hastily recruited from the ranks of British ex-servicemen. Discipline among these forces was non-existent, and tales of their uncontrolled violence still haunt many counties in Ireland.

Home Rule legislation, passed just before the First World War broke out in 1914, provided for an All-Ireland parliament, with some powers reserved to Britain; this plan had been strongly resisted by the Northern Unionists. It had been suspended for the duration of the war, and the British government now set out to revive it, passing the Government of Ireland Act in 1920. This was designed to establish two parliaments in Ireland, North and South. It would copperfasten the existing partition of the country, but unity could be achieved if the two parliaments later agreed to it. The self-government offered was very limited, and important powers would remain under British control, such as law and order, major taxes, and the supreme court. Religious discrimination could

The Irish mission in London at their hotel: Arthur Griffith (on left), Collins (seated third from left). (From The Voice of Ireland, courtesy Central Catholic Library)

not be legalised. The Ulster Unionist Council, which was unenthusiastic about leaving direct British control, finally agreed to a six-county state, within which their voting majority would be two-to-one. They had reluctantly to abandon three counties they had originally wanted to hold on to, Donegal, Cavan and Monaghan.

When the elections for these two parliaments were held in May 1921, Sinn Féin candidates were elected unopposed in every constituency in the south, and formed themselves into the Second Dáil, instead of setting up a Southern Parliament. The Northern Parliament, with Sir James Craig as Prime Minister, was officially opened by King George V on 22 June 1921. The king made an emotional speech pleading for peace and reconciliation, and David Lloyd George, the British Prime Minister, followed up by making approaches to the Dáil.

This caused some surprise on the Irish side, most of whom knew that they could hardly resist the British forces much

"A fateful hour....", artist's impression by Stephen Spurrier of British and Irish delegates at Downing Street conference on Treaty (Illustrated London News)

The Publicity Department of Dail Eireann has issued the following:

'As Minister for Labour it has come to my notice that girls are being dismissed from the tobacco factories at the present time.

'After investigations we are able to say that the enemy are making desperate efforts to recapture the cigarette trade of Ireland, and that our people are gradually being induced to smoke enemy imported cigarettes again.

'I would ask the clubs to take this matter up and get each man to realise that whenever he smokes an English fag he helps to turn an Irish girl adrift on the streets to seek work, hungry and cold, during the coming winter.

'I subjoin a list of Irish cigarettes to help you in getting your local shops to stock them, and I believe that every smoker in Ireland will be able to find a fag to suit his taste among them.

'Minister for Labour.'

Signatures on the Treaty (From The Voice of Ireland, courtesy Central Catholic Library) longer. Many of the officers and more experienced men had been arrested, and the shortage of ammunition was becoming desperate. Collins is said to have remarked later (to the Chief Secretary), 'When we were told of the offer of a truce we were astounded. We thought you must have gone mad'. Lloyd George gambled that the Irish would seem unreasonable if they did not respond to the peace moves, and that the British public might then accept a tougher security policy. De Valera certainly realised that public opinion, Irish and British, would be outraged if Sinn Féin ignored the truce offer.

Lloyd George's offer was made without any conditions this time – earlier offers had demanded the surrender of arms first. He was seriously interested in making peace; he was wary of his army chiefs, who insisted they would need one hundred thousand men, at a cost of £100 million, to achieve victory in Ireland. The vicious activities of the Black and Tans and the Auxiliaries were hardening attitudes among the Irish, and sickening the British public; nothing but stalemate seemed to lie ahead. He was also concerned about international opinion, particularly in the United States, where the Irish-American lobby was very powerful.

De Valera consulted Lord Midleton and other influential Southern Unionists, and a Truce was agreed. Both sides guaranteed to halt movements of troops and displays of force; not to increase officers, men or military supplies; to stop the activities of spies and secret agents; and to avoid disturbing the peace. However, a Sinn Féin boycott of goods from Northern Ireland and Britain, started in August 1920, continued during the Truce, and there was a counter-boycott from the North. The IRA tended to see the Truce as temporary, giving them a breathing-space, and more arms were imported during the six-month Truce than had been in the previous twelve months.

Representatives of the Northern Unionists and of Sinn

Michael Collins at the time of the Treaty negotiations, in serious-minded mood, realising perhaps that the troubles were only beginning (From The Voice of Ireland, courtesy Central Catholic Library)

Féin were now expected to attend a London conference as soon as it could be arranged, but Craig refused to meet Sinn Féin representatives. De Valera visited Lloyd George in London in July 1921, with Arthur Griffith, Robert Barton, Austin Stack and Erskine Childers. After this initial contact, two months of correspondence followed as both sides attempted to agree on common ground. Dáil Eireann was beginning to meet openly, taking advantage of the Truce, and the underground Republican courts which Sinn Féin had established in opposition to the British legal system were now operating in public.

Lloyd George offered Ireland a form of Dominion status, limited by defence restrictions and maintaining partition, but this was rejected by de Valera and the Dáil, who said it gave Ireland less freedom than the Dominion status which Canada already enjoyed. De Valera offered a concept called 'External Association', whereby Ireland would be externally associated with the other Dominions, but would not be a Dominion or within the Empire; she would owe no allegiance to the Crown, and the Irish would not be British subjects. This plan was unacceptable to Britain. Finally, Lloyd George invited de Valera to send delegates to a conference, 'with a view to ascertaining how the association of Ireland with the community of nations known as the British empire may best be reconciled with Irish national aspirations'.

This conference was to see the negotiation and signing of the Anglo-Irish Treaty of 1921.

Northern Ireland

One of the most important subjects to be discussed in the talks was the question of the partitioned North of Ireland. Already volatile, the situation there had worsened under the influence of the War of Independence and the increasing sense of anarchy in the south. Feeling threatened by the rising Nationalist tide across the border, and by Sinn Féin election victories, the Unionist working class and the Ulster Volunteer Force (UVF) were becoming involved in sectarian trouble in several counties in Ulster.

It was Belfast which bore the brunt of the violence. In July 1920, after the Divisional Police Constable of Munster was killed by the IRA, fighting erupted in the shipyards, and Catholic and socialist workers were driven out by a mob. The

violence spread to other workplaces, and the largest ship-
yard firm, although it had abolished its religious test for
workers, had to insist that they sign a declaration designed
by the 'vigilance committee'. A subcommittee sent over by
the British Trades Union Council to investigate despaired of
understanding the situation, and retreated in disorder. In
August, Royal Irish Constabulary District Inspector Swanzy
was murdered in Lisburn, and a curfew had to be imposed.
Nonetheless, Catholic homes and businesses were attacked;
trams were stoned; churches were burned. Rioting raged on
and off for months.

Alarmed by the violence, Craig warned the British gov-
ernment that the loyalist mobs would have to be restrained.
The Ulster Special Constabulary, known as A Specials and
B Specials, had been established in late 1920, but they were
seen as a Unionist force, and never behaved impartially.
During the month of June in 1921, just as the Northern
Parliament was to be officially opened, some RIC men and
Special Constabulary were shot dead, and ten Catholics
were killed in reprisal, while many Catholic families were
driven out of previously mixed streets in Belfast. During the
Twelfth of July celebrations later that year, Specials joined
the Protestant mobs; sixteen Catholics and seven Protestants
were killed. Between June 1920 and June 1922, 1,766 Catholics were wounded and 428 killed; 8,750 were thrown out of
work, and 23,000 forced to leave their homes.

Treaty Negotiations

A surprising aspect of the Treaty conference was that Eamon
de Valera, President of Dáil Eireann, did not attend it. The
Dáil Eireann team which finally went to London in October
1921 consisted of Arthur Griffith, Minister of Foreign
Affairs, Michael Collins, Minister of Finance, Robert Barton,
Minister of Economic Affairs, and two solicitors, E.J. Duggan

and George Gavan Duffy. Erskine Childers, director of Sinn Féin propaganda, acted as Secretary, along with John Chartres and Fionan Lynch.

This group of individuals, bearing such a heavy responsibility, was not very united to start with — Griffith, for example, had a deep dislike and distrust of Childers, who had an English father, but Childers had been specially picked by de Valera to maintain the strict Republican point of view. The three most vehement Republicans in the Cabinet, de Valera, Austin Stack and Cathal Brugha, were left behind.

Why de Valera did not go himself has never been finally explained; possibly he knew a compromise of some sort was inevitable, and did not want to be associated with it, but he may also have felt that he was needed at home, to restrain over powerful Republican emotions in the Dáil. He and Collins had been rivals in authority for some time; certainly, Collins felt that the 'Long Fellow' (de Valera) was deliberately putting him in a difficult position.

It was made clear that although the Irish team were called 'plenipotentiaries', they were not to sign anything without first referring it back to Dublin. De Valera said later that this was intended to give them an occasional breathing-space; if they needed time to think about an issue, they could always say they had to discuss it with their Cabinet colleagues. Besides, proposals could be studied more coolly in Dublin, without the pressure of daily confrontation. The plenipotentiaries were expected to go as far as they could towards a settlement, but never to give way on principles. If they had to come back empty-handed in the end, de Valera would publish whatever the last-ditch proposals had been, and ask whether the British seriously wanted to go to war on what would probably only be a very narrow margin.

Negotiations dragged on over several weeks of haggling, irritation, confrontation, obfuscation, nods and winks. Despite several trips back to Dublin for consultation, with a long and tiring boat-and-train journey each way, the Irish team felt increasingly isolated. They were coming under severe pressure from Lloyd George and the heavyweight British team, which included Lord Birkenhead and Winston Churchill. Thomas Jones, assistant secretary to the British Cabinet, liaised between the British and Irish delegations.

The most important issues to be clarified were a) the exact constitutional status of the new Irish state, b) the question of partition, and c) Britain's concerns about its own military security – access to Irish ports, for example. The Irish delegates had decided to break up the talks, if they had to, on partition. To them this was the issue of greatest importance, and the one which would get them most international sympathy. The British knew this very well, and were determined to prevent it. They concentrated instead on issues of sovereignty; would Ireland pledge allegiance to the Crown? swear an oath? call its citizens British or Irish?

Barton later described the atmosphere as 'strained and formal. The English studied Griffith as the rebel Vice-President but I should say that their interest concentrated upon Collins as the man who had done most to thwart them in the physical force campaign. At that date it must have been unusual for a man with £10,000 on his head to sit at the Downing Street Cabinet table.' Collins, who projected himself as a plain, blunt military man, out of his depth in diplomatic waters, wrote to a friend: 'Either way it will be wrong...You might say the trap is sprung.'

The atmosphere grew more and more claustrophobic, and relations among the delegations were strained to snapping point. Lloyd George held some bilateral discussions with Collins and Griffith only, isolating them from their colleagues, and sowing seeds of suspicion among the other delegates. Griffith knew that compromise was inevitable, but was determined to get as many concessions as he could first.

Cork Weekly Examiner **22.10.21**
On leaving the Conference chamber yesterday, Mr Michael Collins noticed a rifle standing in the corridor. Turning to his colleagues, he humorously asked: 'What is the meaning of this provocative display?'...Mr Lloyd George laughed, and picking up the rifle, explained it was the first American rifle made for the late war. Mr Collins then suggested that he should sit in the chair with the rifle in his hands and that the Prime Minister should send for a photographer...

Sir James Craig, worried about the negotiations, had written to Lloyd George proposing that Ulster should become a Dominion by itself. Lloyd George wanted to offer instead to set up an All-Ireland Parliament, with Ulster having the right to vote itself out within twelve months. If it did vote itself out, then a Boundary Commission would be set up to finalise the northern border. He had originally intended to resign if Craig would not accept unity, but he realised that the Conservative Party, his coalition partners, would not support him, and that Craig was immovable. However, the Conservatives could be persuaded to accept the idea of a Boundary Commission.

In a private meeting with Griffith on 12 November, Lloyd George put the Boundary Commission plan to him, and said that he was going to suggest it as a way of putting pressure on Craig. However, because this suggestion seemed to accept the reality of partition, he could not make it without Griffith's agreement not to contradict it. They must seem to be in agreement, so that Craig would be isolated. Griffith, anxious to move things along, agreed to the document which proposed a Boundary Commission. Surprisingly, he did not realise that it could be read to mean that he accepted the partition of Ireland, and he did not inform the other members of his delegation about this document, apparently not thinking it important enough.

On 25 November, the negotiating team and the Dublin Cabinet, meeting in Dublin, agreed that Ireland could accept the British Crown, for the purposes of the association, as 'symbol and accepted head of the combination of Associated States'; an annual sum of money would be voluntarily voted to the Civil List. The wearied delegates returned to London for the last time. The British Prime Minister had fixed on a deadline of 6 December 1921 by which to send the Irish decision to Craig in Belfast. But deep divisions still existed, among the exhausted Irish negotiators themselves and within Sinn Féin in Dublin.

When negotiations seemed to have hit a wall, Lloyd George played his final card. He triumphantly produced the document which Griffith had agreed to earlier, and claimed that it meant he had agreed to the Boundary Commission and to partition. Griffith, appalled but stung by an appeal to his honour, responded that he would not let the Prime Minister down. The Sinn Féin delegation could not now cut off discussions by using partition as a reason. It later emerged that Lloyd George had assured Craig that a Boundary Commission would leave Unionists with the lion's share of Ulster, while giving the Irish delegation very much the opposite impression; they believed that a plebiscite would be held in the northern counties, leading to ultimate unity.

Lloyd George, bringing matters to a climax, threatened that if he had to send a negative answer to Craig on the negotiations, war would be the result, 'within three days'. They had to come to a decision now on the proposals before them. The Irish delegates seemed to have reached the end of their tether. As they turned to leave for their final consultation, said Churchill, 'Michael Collins rose looking as if he was going to shoot someone, preferably himself. In all my life, I have never seen so much passion and suffering in restraint'.

It seems incredible that they should have signed the final document without contacting the Sinn Féin Cabinet, but they did not even try to telephone. De Valera was out of

Dublin, down in the south-west, and could only have been reached with difficulty; they may have decided that no good could be served by further delay. There was no point in pretending they could go back to full-scale war; the Truce had allowed British troops to come into more friendly contact with the IRA, and to learn more about their resources.

They had also lost another great advantage. Collins, who had escaped capture for years, had been lionised in London and was now a well-known and easily-recognised figure; he could not have gone back to his role as intelligence agent, which had been of crucial importance. He had earlier said to a friend: 'Once a truce is agreed, and we come out into the open, it is extermination for us if the truce should fail'.

Anglo-Irish Treaty

The main provisions of the Treaty (see text p137) gave Ireland the same constitutional status within the British Empire as that granted to the Dominions of Canada and New Zealand, the Commonwealth of Australia and the Union of South Africa. The Free State was to allow the free use of harbour and other facilities to British forces at need (to be reviewed after five years) – Childers protested that this meant that parts of Ireland would remain under permanent British military occupation. Provision was made for a Boundary Commission to be established if the Northern Parliament refused to join the Free State. The Irish Free State would have complete fiscal autonomy.

The oath to be taken by members of the Free State parliament ran as follows: 'I...do solemnly swear true faith and allegiance to the constitution of the Irish Free State as by law established and that I will be faithful to H.M. King George V, his heirs and successors by law in virtue of the common citizenship of Ireland with Great Britain and her adherence to and membership of the group of nations forming the

PROPOSED TREATY OF ASSOCIATION BETWEEN IRELAND
AND THE BRITISH COMMONWEALTH.

In order to bring to an end the long and ruinous conflict between Great Britain and Ireland by a sure and lasting peace honourable to both nations, it is agreed

1. That the legislative, executive, and judicial authority of Ireland shall be derived solely from the people of Ireland.

2. That, for purposes of common concern, Ireland shall be associated with the States of the British Commonwealth, viz: the Kingdom of Great Britain, the Dominion of Canada, the Commonwealth of Australia, the Dominion of New Zealand, and the Union of South Africa.

3. That when acting as an associate the rights, status, and privileges of Ireland shall be in no respect less than those enjoyed by any of the component States of the British Commonwealth.

4. That the matters of "common concern" shall include Defence, Peace and War, Political Treaties, and all matters now treated as of common concern amongst the States of the British Commonwealth, and that in these matters there shall be between Ireland and the States of the British Commonwealth "such concerted action founded on consultation as the several Governments may determine."

5. That in virtue of this association of Ireland with the States of the British Commonwealth citizens of Ireland in any of those States shall not be subject to any disabilities which a citizen of one of the component States of the British Commonwealth would not be subject to, and reciprocally for citizens of these States in Ireland.

6. That, for purposes of the Association, Ireland shall recognise His Britannic Majesty as head of the Association.

7. That, so far as her resources permit, Ireland shall provide for her own defence by sea, land and air, and shall repel by force any attempt by a foreign power to violate the integrity of her soil and territorial waters, or to use them for any purpose hostile to Great Britain and the other associated States.

8. That for five years, pending the establishment of Irish coastal defence forces, or for such other period as the Governments of the two countries may later agree upon, facilities for the coastal defence of Ireland shall be given to the British Government as follows:

    (a) In time of peace such harbour and other facilities as are indicated in the Annex hereto, or such other facilities as may from time to time be agreed upon between the British Government and the Government of Ireland.

    (b) In time of war such harbour and other naval facilities as the British Government may reasonably require for the purposes of such defence as aforesaid.

9. That within five years from the date of exchange of ratifications of this treaty a conference between the British and Irish Governments shall be held in order to arrange for the handing over of the coastal defence of Ireland to the Irish Government, unless some other arrangement for naval defence be agreed by both Governments to be desirable in the common interest of Ireland, Great Britain, and the other associated States.

10. That, in order to co-operate in furthering the principle of international limitation of armaments, the Government of Ireland shall not

    (a) Build submarines unless by agreement with Great Britain and the other States of the Commonwealth.

    (b) Maintain a military defence force, the establishments whereof exceed in size such proportion of the military establishments maintained in Great Britain as that which the population of Ireland bears to the population of Great Britain.

11. That the Governments of Great Britain and of Ireland shall make a convention for the regulation of civil communication by air.

"Document No. 2" – De Valera's counterproposal of 14 December 1921 (from Art Ó Gríofa by Seán Ó Lúing)

British Commonwealth of nations.' The official title of the document, 'Articles of Agreement for a Truce between Great Britain and Ireland', was actually very radical in its implications, because it was a recognition of Irish sovereignty.

Collins predicted that signing the Treaty meant that he was signing his death warrant; yet he signed, as they all did, at 2.10 am on 6 December 1921.

The British were greatly relieved: as Lord Birkenhead later pointed out, 'If there are to be struggles and fisticuffs, then in the first place it ought to be Irish blood and Irish fisticuffs that are expended...I would much rather hear Mr Michael Collins called a traitor by Mr de Valera than hear myself called a traitor by anyone else'. Collins himself wrote to his fiancée, Kitty Kiernan, 'I don't know how things will go now but with God's help we have brought peace to this land of ours – a peace which will end this strife of ours forever'. But as soon as de Valera read the Treaty, he announced that he could not support it.

Prelude To War

The conflict over the Treaty, both inside the Dáil and out, split the country in two. The exhausted delegates defended themselves well in debate, stating that they had got more out of England than anyone in Ireland had ever done before, and that anyway the country had not been in any condition to resume the War of Independence. Griffith proclaimed: 'We have brought back the flag; we have brought back the evacuation of Ireland after 700 years by British troops and the formation of an Irish army...We have brought back to Ireland equality with England, equality with all nations which form that Commonwealth, and an equal voice in the direction of foreign affairs in peace and war'.

Collins maintained that the Treaty provided Ireland with not the ultimate freedom 'that all nations aspire and develop

We sat at a table and watched Dev with a compass finish a very neat drawing he had already begun. There were five separate and independent circles, all contained within a very large circle. Dev completed the design by drawing another circle outside the large circle, but contacting it.

'There you have it,' said Dev, 'the largest circle is the British Commonwealth, having within it these five circles which are members of the Commonwealth. Outside the large circle, but having external contact with it, is Ireland.'

This was the first I had heard of the scheme which came to be known as Document Number Two or External Association...

to, but the freedom to achieve it'. Kathleen Clarke had asked him if he expected people like her to vote for it, but he asserted, 'What I would like people like you to do would be to stand behind us and through your strength ensure that everything promised in the Treaty is got, and then we will work through it to complete freedom'. The Treaty delegates still hoped that they could win agreement, and prevent a final split.

De Valera with others of like mind during the Treaty Debates at the National University Buildings in Earlsfort Terrace (Archives Department UCD)

Kevin O'Higgins stated that the Treaty 'represents such a broad measure of liberty for the Irish people and it acknowledges such a large proportion of its rights, you are not entitled to reject it without being able to show them you have a reasonable prospect of achieving more'. But de Valera had tried to present alternative proposals, which he called 'Document No. 2'. This document contained some aspects of the Treaty, as well as its 'partition' clauses, but it clung to the idea of 'External Association'. It contained no oath of allegiance at all, but said that for the purposes of the Association, 'Ireland shall recognize his Britannic Majesty as head of the Association'. De Valera objected to the Treaty oath as being one of 'allegiance', but he would have had no objection to swearing to be 'faithful'; '...I take it to mean that "faithful" is as regards a bargain made in the faithfulness of two equals who show it in keeping the bargain', he wrote.

Document No. 2 was circulated privately among the Cabinet, but de Valera refused to allow it to be published when it got little support. It was too much of a compromise; one speaker said, 'Do not let us go sideways into the British Empire. If we are going to go in, let us go in with our heads erect and not try to get in dodging around a corner when no one is looking'. And Piaras Beaslaí made an important point: 'There is no alternative to ratification of the Treaty but war. Document No. 2 is no alternative if we must die. Men have died to the cry of "Up the Republic", but I cannot imagine they would die for the cry of "Up External Association"'.

Collins, Griffith and their colleagues and supporters were attacked vehemently, accused of treachery, cowardice and stupidity, of falling for the wiles of the 'Wizard of Wales' [Lloyd George]. Griffith rejected all of this: 'It is for the Irish people – who are our masters, not our servants as some think – it is for the Irish people to say whether it is good enough.' He deplored the appeals being made to past generations and future generations: 'Is there to be no living Irish nation? Is the Irish nation to be the dead past or the prophetic future?'

Constance Markievicz opposed the Treaty on more than Republican grounds: 'My ideal is the Workers' Republic for which Connolly died, and I say that this is one of the things that England wishes to prevent. She would sooner give us Home Rule than a democratic Republic. It is the capitalists' interests in England and Ireland that are pushing this Treaty to block the march of the working people in Ireland and England'. Very little attention was paid to the issue of partition, apart from the fear that the North would be a bridgehead for Britain if it wished to regain control. The issue itself was left to the Boundary Commission to sort out.

The threat of civil war lay behind some of the speeches, especially from those who spoke for the IRA, and other Republicans appealed to idealism: 'We would rather have this country poor and indigent, we would rather have the people of Ireland eking out a poor existence on the soil, as long as they possessed their souls, their minds and their honour,' said Liam Mellows.

When the Treaty was passed on 7 January 1922, with a vote of 64 to 57, de Valera broke down briefly under the stress of emotion, then led his supporters from the Dáil, and prepared to fight the coming 'Treaty election' on the basis of a call for the Republic, and the Republic alone.

7th January 1922 Orders of the Day;

1. Motion by Mr. A. Griffith, T.D. Resolved:
That Dáil Eireann approves of the Treaty between Great Britain and Ireland signed in London on December 6th 1921.

2. Motion by President de Valera. President de Valera will move:
That inasmuch as the 'Articles of Agreement for a Treaty between Great Britain and Ireland' signed in London, December 6th, 1921, do not reconcile Irish national aspirations and the association of Ireland with the community of nations known as the British Commonwealth and can not be the basis of an enduring peace between the Irish and British peoples, DÁIL EIREANN in the name of the sovereign Irish nation, makes to the Government of Great Britain, to the Governments of the other states of the British Commonwealth, and to the peoples of Great Britain and of these several states, the following proposal for a Treaty of amity and association which DÁIL EIREANN is convinced could be entered into by the Irish peoples with the sincerity of good-will.

ove: Dáil Eireann: the Order of Business. **Below:** *Ratification of the Treaty (Topham Picturepoint)*

Chapter 2

Shadows and Uncertainty

Civil War did not start immediately on the acceptance of the Treaty; six months of negotiation, argument and frustration were yet to pass. De Valera resigned as President of the Dáil, therefore of the Republic. Griffith was elected as President of the Dáil, and Collins as Chairman of the Provisional Government, which would stay in office until the legislation putting the Irish Free State in place was passed. The Second Dáil also remained in office, as there was no machinery to abolish it, but it was powerless and without funding.

The job of the Provisional Government was to bridge the gap before a Constitution could be written and accepted, and a full government put in place (if this did not happen within a year, administration would revert to Britain). An Upper House, the Senate, was designed to give Southern Unionists an official voice; this was to make sure that the Treaty would be supported in the House of Lords. The new government was to be concerned only with administrative affairs, and a 'transfer of functions' order enabled it to take over the apparatus of government, both central and local, and about 20,000 civil servants.

British civil servants could be transferred from Dublin to Belfast, on a voluntary basis; about 300 eventually made the move. Senior posts in the Northern Ireland administration were filled by English officials (offered inducements of various kinds), or men of Ulster Protestant stock attracted from departments in London and Dublin. Several departments were excluded from the transfer, among them the Land Commission and the Registry of Deeds. The Northern government was to set up its own Registry of Deeds, and material relevant to the North would then be transferred from Dublin.

The new government was immediately inundated with applications for posts in the civil service and other administrative positions. Widespread canvassing took place of anyone likely to have any influence. New heads were assigned to each civil service department; these included military men such as P.S. O'Hegarty, of the IRB, who took over Posts & Telegraphs. Local rates rose sharply, because of the loss of the £1 million per annum which the Dublin Castle administration had previously provided for local government.

The British government was surprised at the extent of Irish opposition to the Treaty, but they knew that they must not interfere if they wanted the Treaty accepted by the Irish public. A Colonial Office spokesman said: 'The most dangerous weapon the extremists hold is their chance of creating a wave of feeling by committing a series of atrocities which will force intervention and throw us back where we were in 1920'. Winston Churchill was appointed chairman of a Provisional Government of Ireland (PGI) committee, which was to supervise day-to-day issues from London.

In the House of Lords, Birkenhead countered vehement Unionist objections to the Treaty by pointing out that they would have been no better off to continue the war, pouring more men and arms into the country. 'There is no one listening to me who does not know that on the conclusion of that war, with memories a thousand times more bitterly inflamed, Lord Salisbury [opposition leader] would have had to do what we have done now, enter into negotiations with these people and define the conditions under which they and we will live our lives'.

The PGI committee did its best to encourage the insecure Provisional Government, which lacked resources and was unsure of its public support. Kevin O'Higgins later described their position as: '...simply eight young men in the City Hall standing amidst the ruins of one administration, with the foundations of another not yet laid, and with wild men screaming through the keyhole'. Churchill reassured the British House of Commons that the Provisional Government was in full control of the IRA, but privately he was not convinced of this; he was equally unhappy with Collins' aggressive approach to Northern Ireland. The British government now had a much greater appreciation than before of the complexities of the Irish situation; the Treaty negotiations had been an education all round. Widespread unrest led to a rash of strikes – dockers, farm workers, railway workers – and the small Irish Labour Party decided to take

De Valera and his followers withdrawing from the Dáil after the vote to accept the Treaty was passed. (Courtesy Anthony Gaughan). Front row from left: Cathal Brugha, Mrs Margaret Pearse, de Valera, Mrs Kathleen Clarke, Austin Stack.

> ### Clare County Council, December 1921
> '...The people of Clare consider that the Treaty gives us the substance of independence; that it will lead inevitably and within a very short period to the complete fulfilment of our national aspirations, and, therefore, believe that the Treaty should be ratified...
>
> 'Copies of this resolution to be telegraphed to our representatives, President de Valera, Brian O'Higgins T.D., Sean Liddy T.D., and Patrick Brennan T.D.'

> ### Cork Weekly Examiner, 7.1.22
> 'That we, the members of Middleton Urban District Council, unanimously decide to accept the Treaty between England and Ireland as signed by our plenipotentiaries, and call on our own representatives to ratify it.'
>
> '...While cherishing undying gratitude for your services, and appreciation of your position, Roscommon demands with practical unanimity the ratification of the Treaty.'
> V. Rev. Canon Cummins, to E. de Valera

> ### Cork Weekly Examiner, 11.3.22
> At Tipperary No. 1 rural district council,...a resolution was passed calling on the Provisional Government to take active and immediate steps to acquire all available grazing ranches and distribute them among all persons, including I.R.A. volunteers, who had risked their lives in the cause of Irish freedom. Special attention was directed to the large grazing ranches of Ballinard, Lattin, and Mooresfoil...

> ### Cork Weekly Examiner, 28.1.22
> Early on Sunday morning a number of cattle were driven on to the public road off four or five grazing farms in the district of Croom...The farms concerned were, it is understood, let on the eleven months' grazing system, and the object of the drive, it is stated, was to try and have the lands parcelled out amongst cottiers, small holders, and landless men in the surrounding district.

part in the forthcoming Treaty election.

The 'Southern Ireland Parliament' met for the first and only time on 14 January to elect the Provisional Government, with Collins as Chairman. The Dáil was to be dissolved early in March, and the Treaty Election was planned for mid-April. A new Constitution had to be drawn up, and Collins hoped to have the Irish Free State established before that job was completed. Collins' new cabinet included Cosgrave, Duggan, O'Higgins, P.J. Hogan, Joseph McGrath, Michael Hayes, Eoin MacNeill and Fionan Lynch. Griffith, however, remained outside it, as President of Dáil Eireann.

By this stage almost 400 local bodies, such as county councils, farmers' associations and rural district councils, had passed resolutions expressing support for the Treaty.

> **William Irwin,** Betrayal in Ireland
> About this time, too, a new over-printed stamp was on issue. This time the over-print read: 'Saorstat Eireann'. It was recorded all over the city that the first Telegraph Messenger lad to glimpse the new stamp rudely but incorrectly translated it as 'Sore arse Erin'...

Support was equally widespread amongst the general public; birth and marriage announcements were published with 'a hope for many peaceful years', and prayers were raised in church after church.

Republicans were determined that real government control should remain with the Dáil, which was still in existence side-by-side with the Provisional Government. Many of the Dáil ministries no longer functioned in practice, and some of its members attended meetings of the Provisional Government. Duggan, O'Higgins, Cosgrave and Collins were members of both. This dual government created extreme confusion. Each side felt its own position was being weakened, but the situation helped to delay the complete split which would lead ultimately to war. The anti-Treaty group began to issue a propaganda sheet called *Poblacht na hEireann (Republic of Ireland)* under the editorship of Liam Mellows; Erskine Childers later took over this job.

The weight of Collins' responsibilities at this time was unenviable. As Chairman and Minister for Finance of the Provisional Government, he had to set up government departments and take over the administration from the British, as well as establishing a new unarmed police force (the Royal Irish Constabulary was being disbanded), enabling the formation of a new army, and chairing the committee which was drafting the new Constitution. He also acted as PRO for the new government, writing newspaper articles and giving interviews. He visited London (again the tedious boat-and-train journey) over and over again, to confer with the British government, or with Sir James Craig.

Arthur Griffith, elected President of the Executive Council of the Irish Free State
(from The Voice of Ireland, courtesy Central Catholic Library)

As well as the physical efforts, the psychological demands
were immense. He had to keep the British satisfied, without
alienating the Republicans even further, and there was not
even perfect unity within his Provisional Government. He
was becoming more distant from his previous major concern, the IRA, which was showing worrying signs of crisis.
Nonetheless, he was able to make light of his burdens: 'The
stamp on this [letter] was the first Free State stamp ever
licked by a member of the Free State Provisional Government...it was, of course, licked by me for you' (Collins to his
fiancée, Kitty Kiernan, 17.2.22). This is not to suggest that he
was operating singlehandedly; he was leading an energetic
and determined Cabinet, who took on heavy responsibilities
under increasingly difficult circumstances.

At the Sinn Féin annual conference on 22-23 February, the
Provisional Government allowed a compromise to emerge.
The Treaty Election was postponed for three months, and it
was agreed that the new Constitution would be published
beforehand. The government needed this period of truce
very badly, but paid a high price for it. The delay worried
the British, who feared that a Republican-type Constitution
would be drawn up, but Griffith reassured them. The Republicans were also annoyed at the compromise, thinking
that the delay would work to the advantage of the pro-
Treaty side.

First British troops begin to withdraw after 700 years (Cashman Collection RTE)

Ennistymon, Wednesday

...The Black and Tans in charge were busily engaged in packing their goods for removal, and a crowd of children just out from the adjoining school had collected watching the proceedings. It is stated that one of the Black and Tans threw a bomb which landed amongst the children doing much damage. Several of the children were badly wounded by fragments...Those dangerously wounded are Daniel Fitzpatrick, 14 years, and Patrick O'Dwyer, 15 years...

Commandant-General Michael Brennan, I.R.A., has issued a proclamation that in view of...the grave danger of further bloodshed there will be curfew here tonight from 7 o'clock to 5 a.m.

Cork Weekly Examiner, 11.2.22

The Fallen Fortress

That hoary old fortress of feudalism and oppression, Dublin Castle, has fallen!

It has been the dream, nay, the determined aim of different generations of Irishmen, to secure by force of arms its overthrow.

Emmet set forth, having this as his objective; but his efforts ended in failure.

The men of 1916 were equally anxious to capture it; but they, too, were doomed to disappointment.

Now, however, without the firing of a shot, or the blowing of a trumpet, the walls of Jericho have fallen!

The representatives of the Irish Nation merely walked into Dublin Castle, and, hey presto! it was handed over to them.

If the ghosts of the sinister past that haunt this ill-omened institution could speak, what would they say?

Kerry People 21.1.22

Withdrawal of the military from Tralee

... The withdrawal of the military and police from the town [Tralee], with the consequent evacuation of the different barracks, naturally suggests a way of dealing, at least partially, with the housing question, which is a very pressing one for the working population in Tralee. It is believed that the staff barracks in Boherbee will not be used for military purposes under the new regime. It could be turned into an excellent suite of flats in every way suitable for members of the working classes.

Kerry People, 11.2.22

Both de Valera and Collins had forced this compromise. De Valera actually expected that the electorate would vote to accept the Treaty, so he hoped that during the extra three months he could convince the Provisional Government to revise it more to his liking. Collins feared that the election result would lead to a military confrontation, so he was looking for a chance to bring his opponents around to his way of thinking.

However, outside Dublin, Sinn Féin and its authority was disintegrating; pro-Treatyites had stopped attending meetings. The IRA was growing in strength and influence; at the time of the Truce, it had been 3,000 strong, but by November 1921 it had 72,000 members. The new troops were referred to, rather contemptuously, as 'Trucileers', keen to have the name of IRA membership without having actually done any fighting. However, they trained with the best of them, and many of these eager young men were hoping to see some action, and to have their own chance at making history. This trend was very strong in Cork, which had missed out on the 1916 Rising. Veterans of 1916 and the War of Independence were more inclined to favour the Truce than less experienced soldiers.

The IRA was entirely a volunteer army, but the Provisional Government was now going to need a paid, professional defence force. This became another source of discontent, as Collins sent officers around the country offering jobs in the

The new National Army, in the process of taking over from the evacuating British forces (From The Voice of Ireland, courtesy Central Catholic Library)

army and police to influential IRA figures. The IRA tended to distrust all politicians, being convinced that power tended to corrupt, and many of them were disgusted at the sight of friends and relatives rushing to share the 'plums of office'. The idea of a professional army cut across their favourite image of a band of brothers, fighting not for personal gain but for an ideal.

They saw the spreading stain of materialism as a direct result of English influence.

Army Split

One of the first tangible signs of the new order was the removal of British troops from the southern part of Ireland.

De Valera reviewing IRA troops: note volunteer with Thompson machine gun, famous weapon of the1920s, first used widely during Civil War in Ireland (Topham Picturepoint)

This was a matter for celebration; after over 700 years of occupation the old enemy's forces were finally leaving, and the Irish could start running their own affairs. The high point was the day when the keys of Dublin Castle were handed over to Michael Collins on 16 January 1922, and the last troops marched off to the boats. I remember one of my schoolteachers, an elderly nun, describing this day and the sense of jubilation; the light of triumph still shone in her eyes, over forty years later.

As each army barracks was left empty, the IRA moved in, as the official army of the new state. Of course the IRA was also splitting into pro-Treaty and anti-Treaty groups, but the government had no choice but to allow each unit to move into the barracks nearest it, regardless of whether it supported the Treaty or not. This meant that parts of the country began to drift outside government control; anti-Treaty IRA brigades controlled most of Munster, for example. As it happened, the anti-Treaty forces contained some of the most experienced and efficient units of the IRA.

Richard Mulcahy, the Minister for Defence, agreed to the holding of an Army Convention in March, to try to sort out the situation. Meanwhile, however, the Tipperary 2nd Southern Division voted not to recognise GHQ, and raided police and military barracks for arms and equipment. A Free State army had to be established quickly, to counter such activity, but its new officers lacked experience and resources, and mutinies were frequent, usually about grievances of pay and rank. The Free State army was officially established on 31 January 1922, in Beggars' Bush barracks, Dublin, and began training troops to be distributed around the country. It took time; the IRA had been essentially a guerrilla force, and strict army training and discipline had now to be imposed and accepted.

Towards the end of February a crisis arose in Limerick, where rival IRA units fought about the takeover of evacuated British barracks. Michael Brennan, commander in

---

Incident in Tipperary Town

In Tipperary town, a force of old police, while leaving the town in Crossley tenders, were ordered to halt and put up their hands. Firing followed, in which Head-Constable Davis received wounds from which he has died and two others were wounded.
Kerry People 11.3.22

Night dances

In the course of his Lenten Pastoral, Most Rev. Dr O'Sullivan says: '...During the progress of a long and tedious struggle some abuses, as was natural, crept into our midst. Among them is the holding of night dances, especially in country districts...The parents who allow their children to attend these night dances, held very often under no responsible supervision, will have much to answer for before Almighty God...'
Kerry People 11.3.22

Clare, was ordered to occupy the Limerick barracks on behalf of the Provisional Government, but the anti-Treaty forces, under Liam Lynch, got there before him. Brennan appealed for more troops and equipment, and was nervous about the loyalty of some of his own men. However, neither side really wanted a military confrontation, and a settlement was reached. Lynch's troops would remain in two of the military barracks, and the police barracks would be held by Limerick Corporation. This was seen as a defeat for the Provisional Government, and caused alarm in Britain; similar confrontations took place in Offaly and Tipperary.

Griffith was strongly opposed to any compromise with anti-Treaty forces; he was coming to believe that civil war would be inevitable, and he felt that the sooner it came to a head the quicker it would be over. The government now banned the proposed Army Convention, because it was afraid the IRA would declare independence from GHQ. Negotiations took place between Mulcahy and Rory O'Connor, who was calling himself Chairman, Acting Military Council, IRA. O'Connor threatened that the army could prevent an election being held; asked if this meant a military dictatorship, he replied, 'You can take it that way if you like', and claimed that there were times when revolution was justified.

De Valera seemed to be thinking along these lines as well. On 15 March 1922 he announced the formation of a new political party, Cumann na Poblachta, with himself as leader, and made a speech the next day containing the following words: '...if we continue on that movement which was begun when the Volunteers were started, and we suppose this Treaty is ratified by your votes, then these men, in order to achieve freedom, will have to march over the dead bodies of their own brothers. They will have to wade through Irish blood'. He later claimed he had been misrepresented, and had been merely warning of war, not encouraging it.

Top: *Women scouts of the Republican Army (Archives Department UCD)*
Bottom: *Women Scouts of the Republican Army pose for the press (From The Voice of Ireland, courtesy Central Catholic Library)*

At any rate, his influence over the IRA had dwindled away by this time; they were not listening to politicians anymore.

Ignoring the government ban, the Army Convention took place on 26 March 1922, attended by 233 delegates. It reaffirmed the army as Republican, i.e. anti-Treaty, and chose a new Executive of sixteen, which included Liam Lynch (Chief of Staff), Rory O'Connor, Liam Mellows, Liam Deasy and Ernie O'Malley. The Convention revealed very clearly the rifts within the IRA, and when the *Freeman's Journal* printed a detailed account of the proceedings, its presses were wrecked by O'Connor's men. Two days later, the new IRA Executive announced that it no longer accepted the authority of the Minister for Defence, Richard Mulcahy

On 29 March, anti-Treaty forces of the 1st Southern Division (Cork) boarded a British Admiralty vessel, the *Upnor*, as it left Haulbowline, and raided her cargo of arms and ammunition; these were landed at Ballycotton and removed by lorry. This caused great embarrassment on all sides; Collins accused the British forces of having known about the raid in advance and letting it go ahead to undermine the Provisional Government's authority. Churchill reminded Collins that it was now his job to defend the coasts. Around this time, three British officers and a private were kidnapped in Cork, and later found murdered; incidents of this type were happening in many areas.

On the night of 13 April, men of the IRA's No. 1 Dublin brigade, joined later by Tipperary troops, took over the Four Courts in Dublin, the centre of the country's legal system. They proclaimed it as the Republican military HQ, and were led by Rory O'Connor, Liam Mellows and Ernie O'Malley. This group wanted to force the Provisional Government to delay elections indefinitely, to disband the new Civic Guard which was replacing the RIC, and to meet all the IRA's financial needs. O'Malley described the takeover: 'Motorcars and lorries brought in sandbags and barbed wire...The smiling faces one met, the snatches of song at intervals, the ring of voices across the darkness, showed that the men who were tired of the drifting policy now realized that some kind of a decision had been made. We had a good strong headquarters with a well-known name... We had come out into the open; no more hole-and-corner work'.

These were fighting men, impatient of politics and talk, and contemptuous of the uses of democracy. As Michael Collins had once said, many of the younger IRA men felt they had 'arrears to make up', and were determined to snatch at military glory if they could. De Valera, who had not known about this move in advance, issued an impromptu statement, sympathising with the aims of the Four Courts garrison, and extolling their courage: 'In Rory O'Connor and his comrades lives the unbought indomitable soul of Ireland.' He ended with an appeal to the country: 'Irish citizens! Give them support! Irish soldiers! Bring them aid!'

The Four Courts takeover alarmed the British greatly (not to mention the Provisional Government). Churchill warned that if Collins could not deal with the situation, the British might have to, and the PGI committee began to draw up plans for an economic blockade. Not all British troops had been evacuated at this stage; the anti-Treaty IRA raided more barracks, and minor confrontations with the British took place. A more major confrontation in Kilkenny, between pro-Treaty and anti-Treaty Irish forces, resulted in an agreement to share the barracks in the city.

The Provisional Government tried to hold public meetings, to argue their case, but they were constantly heckled by anti-Treaty forces. These forces also damaged roads and railway lines, to prevent public participation. When Griffith planned to address a meeting in Sligo on Easter Sunday, Republican troops poured into the town, but they held back

Sir James Craig (later Lord Craigavon) and Capt. Dixon (later Lord Glentoran) in Dublin, 2 February 1922 (Cashman Collection RTE)

from open conflict. Griffith succeeded in making his speech, protected by MacEoin's pro-Treaty forces.

De Valera was widely assumed to have been behind the Four Courts takeover, although he had been neither informed nor consulted in advance. When a Labour Party delegation pleaded with him to mediate, he would only say, 'The majority have no right to do wrong'. He issued an Easter proclamation, concluding with the words, 'Young men and young women of Ireland, the goal is at last in sight. Steady; all together; forward. Ireland is yours for the taking. Take it'.

Northern Ireland

Meanwhile, across the Border, a combination of sectarian passions, economic hardship and political insecurity was coming to the boil. Encouraged by the instability in the South, the IRA stepped up its campaign to sweep away the new state and unite the island by force. They had taken advantage of the Truce to move forces north. Backs to the wall, suspicious of Britain's intentions, fearing invasion from the South, loyalists reacted violently. Riots in Belfast continued unchecked. IRA political prisoners had been released in December and January, and immediately went back into action; there were at this time about 8,000 IRA fighters in the north.

Eleven IRA men were arrested in Monaghan, on suspicion of trying to release condemned prisoners, and three members of the RIC were kidnapped in retaliation. An IRA incursion into Tyrone and Fermanagh led to the capture of forty loyalists, to be used as hostages; they included an 80-year-old Orange grand master, Anketell Moutray, who sang psalms and 'God Save The King' without stopping until they were released. Unionist passions were further inflamed; this incursion was seen as a deliberate act of war.

The hostages were later released unharmed, after Britain intervened.

On 21 January, Collins and Craig had made a pact which agreed that Catholics in the north would be protected from persecution, and that the South would end its ongoing boycott on northern goods, which had damaged trade. But the IRA considered the border a provocation, and continued raiding and shooting along it. Craig introduced a Special Powers Act, and made the possession of firearms punishable by death. He also appointed Sir Henry Wilson, an arch-Unionist, as his military adviser. As the RIC was being phased out, and the Royal Ulster Constabulary (RUC) had not yet been fully established, the Special Constabulary were in control of security, and operated with great violence and indiscipline. Churchill formed a Border Commission on 16 February, with British, Northern and Southern liaison officers, but it was never effective.

Collins had every intention of destabilising the Northern state in the interests of future unity, and was well aware of most of the IRA activities. He was himself involved in the planning of an attack on the Belfast City Guard. He also organised the transfer of British rifles, which had been supplied to Beggar's Bush barracks, to Anti-Treaty (Irregular) troops, so that he could send the Irregulars' rifles up North. IRA fighters in the North would therefore not be found with the tell-tale British rifles, which could be traced back to his

Above: *Military parade in the new state of Northern Ireland to greet a later Royal visit (Topham Picturepoint)*
Below: *IRA unit on the border during 1922 (Belfast Telegraph)*

command. This meant that he could assure Churchill (without a blush) that no Provisional Government arms would be used in the North.

The Provisional Government took responsibility for the payment of Northern Nationalist teachers who refused to accept grants or paycheques from the new Northern government; the money came from the Secret Service fund. Dozens of schools took up this offer, and over £170,000 was expended to about 800 teachers before the policy was discontinued in November 1922. Ten years later, teachers were still trying to claim 4% of their salaries from the Free State, because the Provisional Government had deducted it for pension contributions, and the Northern state would not give them credit for it.

Northern veterinary inspectors were not recognised by Nationalist cattle-dealers, and were refused co-operation by the Free State Department of Agriculture. 'The [Irish Free State] have at their disposal a complete organisation with a trained staff in the veterinary branch of the department,' said a memo from P.J. Hogan, 'whereas in the six counties there is no such organisation, and it will be exceedingly difficult to establish one, especially if they are forbidden access to office records...' All this obstructionism helped to cripple the North's cattle trade, until the British Agriculture Ministry agreed to accept certificates issued by inspectors from either North or South. Nationalist majority councils also refused to recognise or co-operate with the new state.

One of the most horrific events of this time was the murder of the MacMahon family in Belfast, on 23 March: 'This morning about 1 o'clock I heard the hall door being smashed in. Five men rushed up the stairs and ordered my brothers and myself and Edward McKinney out on the landing. Four of the five men were dressed in the uniform of the RIC but from their appearance I know they are "Specials" not regular RIC...they lined us up in the room below, my father, my four brothers, McKinney and myself, against the wall. The leader said, "You boys say your prayers", and at the same time he and the others fired volley after volley at us...' The narrator, John, and his youngest brother survived; the others did not. In reprisal a Protestant family, the Donnellys, were bombed in their home and shot at; two sons died.

Hundreds of refugees, many of them belonging to the IRA, poured over the border, but the Provisional Government did not want them, and gave them no encouragement to stay. Maud Gonne MacBride (whose son Seán was one of the Four Courts garrison) pleaded with Griffith to provide aid for the refugees, but he retorted: 'The IRA have no right to bring down refugees from the North; it is not our policy, and we are the government'.

Churchill was becoming increasingly irritated by getting letters from Collins complaining about Orange attacks on Catholics, and letters from Craig complaining about IRA border activity. He called the two leaders together, and negotiated a second Craig-Collins pact on 30 March. Efforts were to be made to put Catholic police into Catholic areas, and an advisory committee was to select Catholic recruits for the police. IRA activity would end, expelled families would be brought back to their homes, and political prisoners would be released. The British government would provide a grant of £500,000, one-third for the relief of Catholics and two-thirds for Protestants.

Sir Henry Wilson was enraged by the pact, as were others; a Catholic area of Belfast was raided by police, and five deaths resulted. The aftermath was a trail of outrages and reprisals in Belfast, and the pact collapsed, despite Churchill's best efforts at conciliation.

An IRA offensive seems to have been planned for the North, with the knowledge of Collins and Liam Lynch; volunteers were requested from Southern troops, and finances

Local farmers seek protection from the new Ulster police. (Illustrated London News)

were provided by the pro-Treaty GHQ. However, this offensive failed, owing to poor communications and widespread public knowledge of its intention. The IRA was anyway weak within the North, surrounded by a largely hostile population, and threatened by the British army and the Specials. Besides, Catholics (especially in Belfast) were extremely vulnerable to reprisals. Collins was now being seen as spokesman for Northern Nationalists, and the more politically astute Joe Devlin, the most prominent Northern Nationalist politician, was completely sidelined. He could perhaps have helped the minority population to begin to come to terms with their new situation, but no-one was listening to him.

Collins was blamed for the breakdown of the IRA offensive; it was said that he made quick decisions without thinking them through, and that the aims of the offensive had never been clear. The other government members had

had no idea what was going on, and would have been appalled at the idea of military intervention, but they encouraged the programme of civil disruption devised by their Northern Advisory Committee, which consisted of senior clerics, businessmen and members of the IRA. There seems to have been a general idea, based on ignorance of the Northern situation, that the Unionists would accept unity if British support was withdrawn from them.

The Northern situation worsened daily; the IRA was targeting businesses and community leaders. Railway stations and mills were burnt down, as well as many stately homes; in Desertmartin, Co. Derry, the IRA killed three policemen, and seven Catholics were murdered in reprisal by loyalists before all the Catholic families were driven out

April 1922: Arthur Griffith's handwritten message to the Irish people to stand by the Treaty (from Art Ó Gríofa by Seán Ó Lúing)

of the town. Finally, in May 1922, after a Belfast MP was assassinated, 350 IRA and Sinn Féin members were arrested, and all Republican organisations were banned. A Special Powers Act in April had given the Minister for Home Affairs stringent new powers of detention and sentencing, and the IRA now virtually ceased to operate in the North.

Policy Of Murder

Sectarianism was not confined to the North. An anti-Treaty army officer was shot at a Protestant-owned farm near Bandon, in Cork, on 25 April, and a total of ten Protestants were shot in reprisal over the following week. Some of the murders were distinguished by their ferocity; one horrified letter describes how a young British ex-soldier, who shot the leader of a gang breaking into his uncle's home, had his eyes gouged out by the gang before he was hanged. Protestants began to leave Cork, and other areas of the country where similar attacks took place; refugees headed for the North or for London, where an Irish Distress Committee was set up.

The government naturally condemned this singling out of a group. Griffith said, 'Dáil Eireann...will uphold, to the full extent, the protection of life and property of all classes and sections of the community. It does not know and cannot know, as a National Government, any distinction of class or creed'.

Top: The mine exploded by the retreating Republicans which destroyed the Public Record Office and the rere of the Four Courts hangs a cloud of smoke over the river Liffey (Cashman Collection RTE) **Below**: Mansion House meeting on 8 May 1922 of IRA and National Army leaders trying to avert civil war: from left to right: Sean MacEoin, Sean Moylan, Eoin O'Duffy, Liam Lynch, Gearoid O'Sullivan, and Liam Mellows (Cashman Collection RTE)

Chapter 3

Fire Over the Four Courts

The prospect of a civil war grew closer; fears were being expressed by church figures and labour leaders. A meeting of Catholic bishops in Maynooth at the end of April came out firmly in support of the Treaty, and condemned anyone who would take up arms against it. The IRB tried to bring the IRA together again, and a joint meeting of the Supreme Council and the divisional centres was held on 19 April 1922.

The majority opposed the Treaty, despite Collins's efforts, but a committee was appointed to try to prevent war. However the anti-Treaty IRA leaders in the Four Courts refused to co-operate, and the committee got nowhere. In Sinn Féin, only 117 out of over a thousand clubs were fully paid up, and it was only in the counties around Dublin that any kind of organisation still existed. The IRA were working against the separate political structure.

The Labour Party had many social and political opinions in common with the anti-Treaty groups, but it recommended neutrality to its followers; Tom Johnson, its leader, was anxious to keep his party away from unconstitutional politics. A general strike on 24 April, in which 75,000 workers took part, was a protest against militarism and the prospect of war. To many people it seemed a substitute for a definite Labour Party policy towards the Treaty. The labour movement as a whole was infected by the unrest in the country, and by the economic situation; the unemployment rate was 25 per cent. Crime of all types increased, particularly armed robbery. Farmers were withholding land-purchase annuities, and cattle-stealing was becoming widespread.

Over eighty groups of workers established 'workers'

Ulster outrages: Sinn Féin murders of Protestant farmers in South Armagh, drawing by H. Raven Hill (Illustrated London News)

soviets' during 1922, taking over factories and creameries and running them on co-operative lines. They were all disowned by the Irish Transport and General Workers' Union, which found itself being sued for damages by angry owners. The Provisional Government's Department of Labour was kept extremely busy. Conciliation boards were established, but the Department did not feel confident enough to deal firmly with strikers until the closing stages of the Civil War.

The history of the soviets is obscure, but they show there were groups in Ireland which were interested in wide sociological issues, and in the type of society the Irish Free State might become. However, they were condemned by the Irregulars, the Free State and the owners alike, and accused of stirring up workers to violence. None of the soviets remained in operation for long.

A statement published by some Army officers on 1 May proposed an acceptance of the Treaty, a non-contested election, and the formation of a coalition government. The Four Courts Executive denounced it, but it helped to start a peace process in the Dáil. Harry Boland produced a statement on the Republican viewpoint which insisted that the Dáil should remain as the government, and that the Treaty issue should be decided by an election. A Dáil committee, chaired by Kathleen Clarke, continued talks until 17 May, but without real hope of success.

Frank Aiken, in charge of the 4th Northern Division of the IRA, appealed to leaders on both sides to come together to protect the Catholics in the North. Collins responded in the Dáil, saying that the British would return if the Irish started 'slaughtering each other', and de Valera agreed with him on the need for stable government. For three days the two men were locked in discussion, and on 20 May, Eamon de Valera and Michael Collins signed an Election Pact, much to everyone's astonishment.

Credit for much of this would seem to belong to Harry

Boland, a long-time close friend of both men, and the terms
of the Pact reflected his earlier proposals. There was to be a
national coalition panel of Sinn Féin candidates for the election, agreed by the candidates themselves, and the number
of candidates on the panel would reflect the strength of each
party in the Dáil (86 pro-Treaty, 58 anti-Treaty). Non-Sinn
Féin candidates could also stand, of course. After the election, a coalition government of nine Sinn Féin members
would be formed, with membership of five to four in favour
of whichever Sinn Féin group won the most votes. If this
coalition broke down, there would be a general election. The
Treaty was not referred to in the Pact at all, nor was the
Constitution. This was an arrogant theft of the people's right
to decide; voters were not to be told whether they were
voting for pro- or anti-Treaty Sinn Féin candidates, and the
politicians would sort it all out for them later.

The Pact was approved by Sinn Féin at its Ard-Fheis
(conference): Collins announced, to cheers, that 'Unity at
home is more important than any Treaty with the foreigner,
and if unity could only be got at the expense of the Treaty –
the Treaty would have to go'. Griffith, who had not been
consulted, is said never to have called Collins by his Chris-
tian name again; he saw the Pact and the election panel as a
denial of the democratic right of the people. They would be
forced to vote by party, not on the issue of the Treaty itself.

The British government was appalled; a complete care-
fully-balanced edifice seemed to have come crashing down.
Churchill pointed out that the whole effect of the Pact was
to monopolise power for Sinn Féin, and to prevent the

electorate from expressing its opinion on the Treaty. It would break Article 17 of the Treaty, which said that every member of the new government would have to accept the Treaty in writing. How could anti-Treaty TDs sign that? He refused to hand over any more arms to the Provisional Government, and halted the evacuation of British troops.

But Britain was in a cleft stick. If they responded too aggressively, they would be accused by international opinion of not having seriously meant to give Ireland independence at all, and jumping in at the smallest excuse. The Irish could also claim that the British were expecting miracles – how could they stabilise a demoralised country overnight? They had to be given a chance to try, without British interference.

Craig was furious with the Pact, seeing it as undermining the Treaty, and he prophesied a civil war between North and South. He immediately announced that his government would not deal with any Dáil elected in this way, nor would

Collins and Harry Boland at Croke Park in happier days (from Michael Collins by Piarais Beaslaí)

he co-operate with it in a Boundary Commission. There was an outbreak of shooting and bombing in Belfast, and Catholic refugees began to stream across the Border again.

Collins' reasons for agreeing this Pact are still unclear, but he was desperate for a breathing-space in which the Constitution could be completed, and felt this was the only way the election could take place at all in such an uneasy atmosphere. The Provisional Government could not protect every single polling station, and the election could have been invalidated by IRA attacks. He also wanted to concentrate on the Northern situation, free from conflict in the Dáil. The Pact would probably work for the pro-Treaty side in the end. De Valera's only chance of gain would be if the new Constitution could be published before the election took place, and was satisfactory to both sides.

Many on the Republican side were unhappy with the Pact, although it could be seen as a tactical victory for them, as it was bound to return more anti-Treaty candidates than their actual support seemed to deserve. But the Pact demonstrated the weakness of de Valera's position, and his desperate attempts to maintain an influence over events. He still hoped to force revision of the Treaty, perhaps reviving the idea of External Association. Seeking even further delay in the election, he demanded the updating of the electoral register (which admittedly dated back to 1918, and did not take account of recent advances in women's voting rights), but this was rejected by Griffith.

The signing of the Pact increased the chances of reunification in the Army, and talks began to make headway. A new Army Council was proposed, but difficulties arose in deciding its membership, and the Four Courts Executive finally rejected all the proposals. In hindsight, anti-Treaty leaders felt that the Provisional Government had only been playing a delaying game with the talks, while it worked away at forming its inexperienced troops into a professional army. Everything now hinged on reaction to the Constitution, which was nearing completion.

The British government were anxious to see the Constitution before the Treaty Election. They feared that its emphasis might be more republican than the Treaty allowed, and they were afraid of a united South making a concerted attack on the North. The Constitution Committee, beginning its work in January 1922, had concentrated on defining the democratic authority of the Free State, and had ignored the issue of Anglo-Irish relationships. The final draft of the Constitution eliminated the Oath to the Crown, and did not mention the Crown's executive authority. It said, 'The legislative, executive and judicial authority of Ireland shall be derived solely from the Irish people', and another clause stated that only the Free State Government could declare war on behalf of the country.

Of course none of this was acceptable to Britain, or bore much relation to the agreed Treaty. Collins was summoned to London after the Pact was signed, and informed that the draft constitution would have to be altered to acknowledge the authority of the Crown, to include an Oath, and to recognise Northern Ireland. The Provisional Government could appease de Valera, or support the Treaty, but not both.

In the end the Irish Cabinet stuck by the original Treaty, although the amended draft Constitution still underplayed the role of the Crown – the Free State Executive Council was to be appointed by Crown representatives, but only after nomination by the Dáil. The outward forms were preserved, and this was what mattered most to Britain, and to the Provisional Government. Parliament would convene and have its executive function in the name of the King. If conflict arose between the Constitution and the Treaty, precedence was to be given to the Treaty.

But the Constitution went much further than those of other Dominions in terms of autonomy; the Governor-

General (who represented the Crown) would be nominated by the Provisional Government, and would have no powers to dissolve the Dáil. The Senate was to be enlarged and strengthened. It is worth noting that the new Constitution contained universal franchise for all men and women over 21, six years before British women between 21 and 30 were given the vote.

Just before the election, in early June, a dangerous clash took place between Irish and British troops in the neighbouring villages of Pettigo and Belleek, which straddled the border. There had been sporadic fighting between the IRA and the Specials in the area, and the IRA succeeded in seizing both villages when Free State troops left Belleek Fort. Churchill, enraged by reports that Provisional Government troops were involved, sent British troops to recover the villages, using artillery on Pettigo. Three Free State soldiers were killed. Collins demanded a joint enquiry into the affair, insisting that his troops had had nothing to do with any aggression, although they had been in the area, and complaining of 'unwarranted interference with our forces in our territory'. The episode undermined trust still further.

Election

Election day was 16 June 1922, and the Constitution was not published until that very morning, apparently for technical reasons. It would probably not have made much difference to the result of the election, but its late publication aroused all sorts of fears and suspicions among the Republican side. It now seemed extremely unlikely that a coalition government could be formed, no matter what the election results were; all the members of the government would have to take the oath under the new Constitution, and the Republicans would not.

The panel system for the election did not work in the end.

Above: *The precipitating event: the assassination of Field-Marshal Sir Henry Wilson, military advisor to the Northern Ireland government. Illustration by Stephen Spurrier (Illustrated London News)*

Left: *Rory O'Connor, the engineer turned Republican leader, whose occupation of the Four Courts in imitation of 1916 posed a threat to the new government, photographed at the time of the split (From The Voice of Ireland, courtesy Central Catholic Library)*

The attitude of each Sinn Féin candidate to the Treaty was made clear by the newspapers, and as proportional representation was being used (for the first time in a general election) the public were in fact able to vote on the one issue, that of support for the Treaty.

Non-Sinn Féin candidates (all, as it happened, pro-Treaty) had been allowed for in the Pact, but they later complained of widespread and persistent intimidation. Some election agents were kidnapped, and there were complaints of personation. Farmers' Party and Ratepayers' Party candidates were attacked, and some withdrew. The moral pressure was intense. Indeed, Collins and de Valera had issued a joint statement regretting the involvement of non-Sinn Féin candidates: 'in view of the fact that one of the most obvious aims of the agreement was the avoidance of electoral contests which could not fail at present to engender bitterness and promote discord and turmoil, the signatories had hoped that the spirit of the pact would have ensured that such contests would be reduced to a minimum'.

The Pact was finally scuppered by Collins himself, two days before the election, when he said in Cork: '...I am not hampered now by being on a platform where there are Coalitionists. I can make a straight appeal to you...to vote for the candidates you think best of, who the electors of Cork think will carry on best in the future the work they want carried on...You understand fully what you have to do, and I depend on you to do it'. This speech was not widely publicised, and in another speech the following day he urged voters to support the Pact in the spirit in which it was made. However, it was clear that it no longer mattered; the Constitution that had been agreed meant that coalition government would be impossible.

The election brought out a very large non-Sinn Féin vote, and a huge pro-Treaty majority. The people wanted peace, and were primarily interested in economic and social stability. Of the 620,000 votes cast (a turnout of just less than 60%), 239,193 went to pro-Treaty Sinn Féin candidates (58 seats), 133,864 to the anti-Treaty side (36 seats), and 247,276 to non-panel candidates, who were all pro-Treaty (34 seats). Farmers' Party candidates were successful in all but one of the constituencies they stood for, and the Labour Party won 29.4 per cent of the vote, with 17 seats, astonishing itself; the labour movement was in healthier shape than it had thought. More than 78% of the poll had voted for the Treaty.

In the light of the impending Civil War, it is interesting to note the distribution of anti-Treaty votes, less than 22% overall of first preference votes. Anti-Treatyites won 5 out of 44 seats in Leinster, and did badly in the three Ulster counties and in Cork city. Connaught produced a small anti-Treaty majority, and Munster a small pro-Treaty majority. The prospect of a coalition government was now minimal, but de Valera continued to hope that Collins would stick by the Pact.

The British government felt that now the Provisional Government had the democratic backing it had needed, it was time to get tough with the dissidents. At this critically important time Sir Henry Wilson, who had headed security policies in the North and had been appalled by the Treaty, was shot and killed in London, on 22 June. His assassins, two IRB men, were arrested and subsequently executed, despite attempts to rescue them.

This reasons for this assassination are still a matter of controversy, but the available evidence seems overwhelmingly to point to Collins's orders. Wilson had been the 'tough man' in the North, and fiercely opposed to Collins, and his death would be a sign to Northern Nationalists that they had not been forgotten. It is possible that Collins had issued an early order to kill Wilson, but had later meant to countermand it; it certainly occurred at a bad time for the Provisional Government, and placed it in a very weak position in relation to British demands for action. But it seems that to Collins the Northern situation took precedence over everything, even the Treaty, and he continually took enormous political risks by involving himself in cross-Border activities.

The Four Courts garrison was blamed for the Wilson assassination (however unlikely this seemed, even at the time), and Collins was put under enormous pressure by the British to take final action to dislodge them from their positions in Dublin city centre. These included such buildings as the Ballast Office, Kilmainham Jail, and much of O'Connell Street. An IRA split at the Army Convention of 18 June had already weakened the Four Courts Executive. Liam Lynch had made proposals for unity which were rejected. Tom Barry had then proposed that unless all British troops left Dublin within 72 hours, they would be attacked. When this was also rejected, about half the delegates left to join the Four Courts garrison. Twelve out of the sixteen IRA Executive members were now in the Four Courts.

The British government was laying plans to attack the Four Courts themselves, if the Provisional Government would not, but drew back from actually carrying this out. It was obvious that the results of such interference would have been disastrous, but practicalities were briefly swept aside by anger and impatience, and by corroding doubts about the Provisional Government's reliability. Churchill made a stirring speech, stating that if the siege was not ended, '...we shall regard the Treaty as having been formally violated, that we shall take no steps to carry out or legalise its further stages, and that we shall resume full liberty of action in any direction that may seem proper...' The *Times* said that: 'The moment has at last come for Mr Collins to choose which path he shall take. There are only two paths – that of the Treaty and that of anarchy'.

It seems that the Provisional Government finally decided to move on 26 June. The following day Leo Henderson, leader of a republican raiding party, was arrested by Free State troops, and in retaliation the Four Courts garrison

Free State troops closing the ring on the Republicans behind the Four Courts (Cashman Collection RTE)

kidnapped J.J. O'Connell, the Free State deputy chief of staff. This served to justify the decision to attack which had already been taken. Griffith and his ministers had to affirm their democratic right to govern, and many of them had been impatient at the delays in confronting the Republican garrison. They could not do anything without military support, but once Collins had accepted the necessity, the attack could go ahead. Collins was deeply reluctant to attack men who had once been his friends, but he had no other choice. In hindsight, it might have been better simply to let the siege run, preventing supplies reaching the garrison until they were forced to surrender, but the pressure for an authoritative gesture was too great.

Meanwhile, unknown to the government, the IRA split had been healed. Full Executive meetings were being held again, and indeed Liam Lynch left the Four Courts only a few hours before the final attack. He was arrested on his way south, but released, because Mulcahy did not realise the Army had reunited, and hoped that Lynch would be an influence for peace. The Four Courts men (supported by the women's arm of the Irish Volunteers, Cumann na mBan) do not seem to have expected an attack, and did not take adequate defensive measures. No-one wanted to fire the first shot in what might be a Civil War, but they were not inclined to surrender either. O'Malley describes the situation: 'They opened the Bridewell gates, opposite the Headquarters block across the street, and marched in...Our position was being slowly surrounded..."We're like rats in a trap, Paddy," I said to O'Brien'.

There was no proper contact between the Four Courts Executive and members of the No. 1 Dublin Brigade outside, and almost no communication with IRA units outside Dublin. The Republican political leadership had no idea what was going on at all, and matters had been made worse by the earlier split in the anti-Treaty ranks at the Army

Convention. Leadership within the Four Courts was also confused; Paddy O'Brien of the No.1 Brigade was Officer Commanding, but the Executive leadership was represented by Joe McKelvey (Chief of Staff), Liam Mellows and Rory O'Connor.

The attack on the Four Courts began on 28 June, after a request to surrender had been rejected, and lasted three days. The British army had lent two 18-pound guns, but there were no experienced gunners among the Free State troops, and they were short of ammunition; the British were still wary of handing over large supplies of munitions, although Churchill was keen to do so. The Provisional Government had to be careful about accepting assistance from the British, because of the propaganda victory this would be for the anti-Treaty side. Even so, mocking verses were being heard on Dublin streets:

England gave the orders, and gave the cannon too
And Michael sent the boys in green to conquer Cathal Brugha
For England's bloody vengeance must be satisfied anew
For England gave the orders, and gave the cannon too.

The Four Courts garrison refused to surrender, despite the bombardment and the appalling conditions, and finally detonated two mines in their munitions centre, the archives department. Most of the contents of the Public Record Office were destroyed, an irreplaceable loss for Irish historical research. They included, of course, massive numbers of documents relevant to Northern Ireland, which had not yet been transferred north.

Finally Oscar Traynor, who commanded the anti-Treaty troops outside the Four Courts, insisted on a surrender, and Mellows, O'Malley and O'Connor were forced to agree. O'Malley described the scene: 'The machine-gunners stripped their guns, jumped on the parts, twisted and battered them; their hands were torn and bleeding but they did not heed, they smashed in a frenzy... The rifles and revolvers were heaped in a large room... Paraffin was slopped around the floor, and then with blinding flashes incendiary grenades were thrown; flames flared on the rifle pyre, licking the butts and the woodwork. We watched for a time, tears of rage in our eyes'. The fighting in Dublin city centre continued till 5th July, and the Irregulars were driven out of one building after another. At least £3 million worth of property was destroyed; shops closed, terrified people hid in their homes, and communications outside the city were cut off.

Maud Gonne MacBride, hoping to help in peace moves, brought together a large group of politically active women, ranging from suffragettes to trade unionists. They visited both Arthur Griffith and Oscar Traynor, claiming, as Mrs MacBride said, 'as women, on whom the misery of civil war would fall, that we had a right to be heard'. They proposed a cessation of fighting, but Griffith refused to accept any terms: 'We are now a government and we have to keep order'. As the noise of the fighting died away in Dublin, it was clear that a Civil War had begun.

> O Churchill dear and did you hear the news from Dublin town
> They've listened to your good advice and blown the Four Courts down
> And likewise with O'Connell Street, the like I've never seen
> And guns (the best) as per request, and lorries painted green.

"Let's play soldiers": boys parading outside the sandbagged Four Courts before
the fighting starts (Fitzelle Album National Library of Ireland)
"Easter Week Repeats Itself" – poster puts the positions of the two sides
graphically (Hulton Deutsch)

Above: Republican barricades were thrown across streets around their strongholds on the north side of the city (National Library of Ireland)
Left: Child (to soldier on duty at Street Barricade): "Mother says will ye give us the bed and she'll let ye have the kitchen table." (Dublin Opinion August 1922)

Opposite Page: Irish Free State Volunteers "having a sup" during a pause in the fighting (National Library of Ireland)
BP lorry with Irish Free State Volunteers (National Library of Ireland)

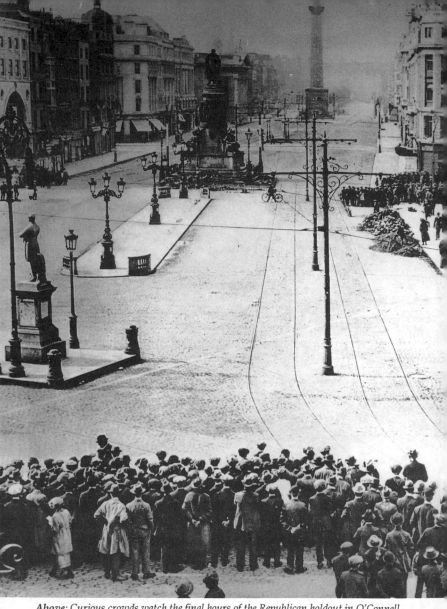

Above: Curious crowds watch the final hours of the Republican holdout in O'Connell (Sackville) St (Topham Picturepoint)
Opposite top: Removing civilian wounded from tenements (Cashman collection RTE)
Middle: The white flag is flown: Republicans prepare to surrender in O'Connell (Sackville) St (National Library of Ireland)
Bottom: Fr O'Reilly leads civilians to safety in the Marlborough St Model Schools (Cashman Collection RTE)

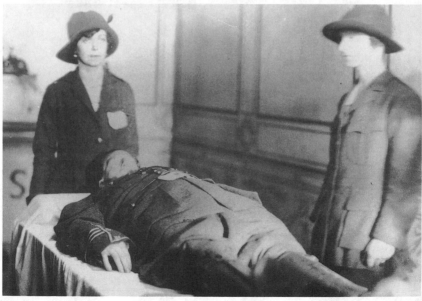

Above: Ruins of the
Gresham (Cashman
Collection RTE)
Right: "Arrived all right.
Am staying at the
Gresham." (Dublin
Opinion)

Opposite Top: The ruins
of the Four Courts from
Inn's Quay, with Free
State troops searching
suspected civilians
(National Library of
Ireland)
Bottom: Cathal Brugha
lying in state in Mater
Hospital (Cashman
Collection RTE)

Above: Free State soldier searching civilian for arms in St Mary's Lane after the fall of the Four Courts and the Republican retreat (Cashman Collection RTE)
Below: Crowds inspect the ruins in O'Connell (Sackville) St (Murtagh Collection RTE)

CHAPTER 4

The Civil War

The lead-in to the Irish Civil War was prolonged and complicated, and it lived long in the collective memory, but the actual war was brief, and could be described in a few lines. In the early stages, severe fighting took place, as Irregular troops took over towns and barracks, but they were gradually driven from their fortified positions, and the war moved into a guerrilla phase of ambushes and reprisals. The total casualty list, by May 1923 when arms were dumped, amounted to between 500 and 800 Free State troops killed, and probably rather higher casualties among the Irregulars, but there are no precise figures. And there are no reliable figures for civilian deaths and injuries, either.

There had been considerable damage to buildings, roads, bridges and railway lines during the War of Independence, and the Civil War added at least a further £30 million to these losses. War materials, armaments, etc. cost the state around £17 million. Prisoners had to be housed, dependants' allowances had to be paid, and meanwhile rates and taxes went uncollected in many areas. Communications were destroyed, trade and industry were severely damaged, and many businesses collapsed. This was an appalling financial burden for a young state, trying to establish a working administration and hoping to encourage investment from overseas.

Another enormous cost was the loss of the talent and energy of those who died during the war, who emigrated after it in despair, or who remained forever alienated from the new state. Long-term enmities resulted both from official executions and from wartime atrocities, committed by both sides. Brutalities cut far more deeply when they were inflicted by Irishmen upon Irishmen, instead of by a foreign foe.

The tragedy of a country suffering a civil war is perhaps best shown in the death of Harry Boland, who was shot in July 1922, dying in great agony in hospital four days later. He had been a member of the IRA and the IRB, and had long been a friend of both de Valera and Collins. He had acted as mediator for their electoral pact, but had finally sided with de Valera on the Treaty. When Boland died de Valera's secretary recorded, 'He felt it terribly – crushed and broken. He lost his most faithful friend'. Meanwhile Michael Collins was passing the hospital where Boland lay: 'My mind went in to him lying dead there and I thought of the good times together and whatever good there is in any wish of mine he certainly had it...I'd send a wreath but I suppose they'd return it torn up'. He could not, of course, attend the funeral.

War Tactics

The Provisional Government set up a War Council on 12 July 1922. Sean MacEoin took over the Western Command, and Eoin O'Duffy the Southern Command. Emmet Dalton commanded in the East, and J.T. Prout in the South-East. J.J. O'Connell headed the Curragh forces. Several government members, such as Collins, took up military duties, and their administrative responsibilities were shared out among the other cabinet members. A directive to the press laid down that the state's army was to be called the 'Irish Army' or

The border village Pettigo, with the last British flag there on display: one of the flashpoints in clashes between Republicans and the new Northern government forces (From The Voice of Ireland, courtesy Central Catholic Library)

Free State troops at Killaloe, moving on Limerick during the drive towards the southwest from Dublin (National Library of Ireland)

Ernie O'Malley's Arrest

At about half past seven next morning, 4 November, Sheila tapped hard at my door. I was awake at once as my habit was when anything unusual was to happen.

'Earnan, the house is surrounded; the Staters are coming in the gate. Mama saw them outside as she was coming back from Mass. Are you all right?'...I heard heavy knocks at the front door and the sound of feet going downstairs, whilst I dressed in the darkness, putting my trousers and coat over pyjamas. My hand was shaking but my mind was clear as I moved the .45 cartridges in rows of six on the table beside the bed. Then I put a cardboard file of my most important papers on a chair. I would bring them with me if I broke through, or burn them in a bucket which I kept in the room for that purpose....

They were in Mrs. Humphrey's room, now, at the end of the corridor.... I heard Mrs. Humphreys say: 'Oh, that's a clothes press,' as the curtains were drawn back.

A rifle butt crashed against the wooden partition.

A man's voice said: 'It's hollow.'

My heart beats were now so loud in the darkness that I felt they must be heard outside, and I pressed one hand hard against my heart to keep it quiet, but it seemed to be now on top of my tongue. I had moved to one side of the door to avoid bullets, and had already shifted the dressing table to make a slight barricade.

Rifle butts crashed in shattering echoes; a panel began to give way, a portion of another splintered, showing a little light; a piece of wood fell into my room. I thought of firing through the door, releasing the spring and rushing out, but Mrs. Humphreys might be behind the Staters. Another panel was smashed in, but those outside could not see anything yet in the darkness. They had not located the hidden spring. I heard the men breathing hard as they struck in the narrow corridor. I would have to fire. I could not wait for a grenade to be thrown in. A heavy crash; the door swung open and a hand appeared. I fired twice; once at the hand, then below and to the right at what might have been the body, and there was a cry of pain. I heard a rush of feet, but I was afraid to fire again as some of the family might be in my way.

As I came out of the room I saw the attackers scrambling out of the hall like frightened sheep. I saw a chin edged out from a door. Another of them, I thought as I fired. There was a thud. I fired again close to the corner and rushed forward. Miss O'Rahilly lay on the floor, blood on either side of her cheeks. She was pale but she did not moan. I had shot her through the chin.

'O my God, I've shot you; that's terrible,' I said. 'I thought I'd got a Stater and it's you.' (Shortly afterwards O'Malley was captured.)
From *The Singing Flame* November-December 1922

> ### The 18-pounder
> ...The 18-pounder was brought up...'Now do you see that wood? That's our target,' [Hales] said...'Now load it with a blank shell.' And someone said, 'Are you mad? A blank shell?' 'I'm not mad,' he said. 'A blank shell will do. I don't want to kill any of the poor devils.' They're the words he used. I'll never forget it. He had two brothers fighting on the other side.
> John L. O'Sullivan, in Griffith & O'Grady (eds), *Curious Journey*

National Army', and that their opponents were always to be referred to as 'Irregulars' or 'bands'.

The IRA troops who had taken over the Four Courts and other buildings in Dublin seem to have had little idea what their next move would be. They were making the same mistakes as the rebels of 1916; once forces are trapped in one place, unable to move around, they will inevitably be bombed out or starved out, or will simply get fed up and demand some action. The IRA Council members who had not joined the Four Courts garrison had decided it was a dead-end tactic, and wanted to concentrate instead on guerrilla fighting, at which their men were skilled.

The Labour Party produced a peace initiative, which de Valera seemed to support, but the Provisional Government demanded the surrender of arms before any talks, and this was refused. De Valera himself decided to return to the Third Battalion IRA, where he had previously served, as a private; he had lost any control over events now. He was posted to the Hammam Hotel, in O'Connell Street, from which he escaped during the fighting, and was later made Adjutant to Sean Moylan, Director of Operations. He remained an important figure, but had no decision-making power.

One by one the occupied buildings in Dublin were picked off by the Free State troops, and the Republican forces (gradually becoming known as the 'Irregulars') decided to evacuate the city. As they retreated from the Hammam Hotel Cathal Brugha, one of the bravest fighters of the War of

Makeshift barricades in Upper William Street, Limerick (National Library of Ireland)

Independence and a vehement speaker during the Treaty debates, ran out of the building last of all, firing as he went, and was shot down. Collins later said, 'Because of his sincerity I would forgive him anything', but Ernie O'Malley's comment was: 'He had preferred death rather than outlive the dishonour of his former comrades. That, to me, was a policy of desperation, and it was unsoldierly. Dying to carry out orders in a job of work was one thing, seeking death was a different idea.'

The Irregular leadership had been greatly weakened by the Four Courts surrender. Rory O'Connor and Liam Mellows were now in prison; so was Tom Barry, who later escaped, and Brugha was dead. O'Malley and Sean Lemass escaped immediately after their arrests, and Liam Lynch and Liam Deasy managed to reach the south, where they co-ordinated the anti-Treaty forces. Lynch took over as Chief of Staff, and ordered all troops to return to their command areas. Much to the relief of Churchill and Birkenhead, the Dublin fighting ended without needing the intervention of the British troops which were still in the city.

The Third Tipperary Brigade

The gun-crew took turns carrying the gun. The Lewis, weighing about 33 lbs, was carried on the shoulder. Thus a man's coat became frayed at that spot. One man of 8th Battalion, when captured, was asked what section he belonged to. 'The Red Cross,' he replied. 'I suppose,' remarked the old ex-British soldier questioning him, 'It was carrying the bandages that wore that hole in your coat?'

C. Conway, 'TheThird Tipperary Brigade'

Visitor: "I wish to interview Lieutenant-General Michael J. O'Regan, the Officer Commanding in this area."
Sentry: "Hey there, Mike, you're wanted!"

Visitor: "I wish to interview Lieutenant-General Michael J. O'Regan, the Officer Commanding in this area." Sentry: "Hey there, Mike, you're wanted." (Dublin Opinion)

Robert Brennan, *Allegiance*

...The vociferous lady who had been on the ship's tender came in and sat at a table, to the music of peals from her golden bangles. She immediately launched out. She was coming back after twelve years to see her people in Limerick, though she wouldn't have come back if she didn't have to. And what was her welcome? No buses or trains. The roads all blocked, the bridges all blown up. She was talking to the waiter and, as he did not reply, she asked him point blank: 'Don't you think this is a scandalous war?'

'God damn it,' he said, 'sure it's better than no war at all anyway.'

The Irregular forces, in most areas of the country, found that they were fighting without local support, which had been vitally important during the War of Independence. People were anxious for peace, willing to give the Provisional Government a chance, annoyed at these malcontents who were stirring up trouble again. Another problem for Irregulars was that although they were fighting on familiar territory in their own localities, they were fighting ex-comrades, who were well aware of their hiding places and personnel.

The Civil War, in fact, seemed to have taken everyone unawares. No-one had been planning for it, or discussing tactics, or laying in supplies. The Free State army was hardly in a condition to fight, still consisting mainly of half-trained and inexperienced men. The Irregulars had managed to hold on to a number of army barracks, but they were short of guns, ammunition and money, and had to resort to raiding banks and post offices, and attacking police barracks.

Communications among the Irregulars were difficult, and depended largely on the women of Cumann na mBan, who acted as drivers and couriers throughout the war. Cumann na mBan had held its own Convention on 5 February 1922, and the vote had gone 419 to 63 against the Treaty. Constance Markievicz was elected President, and pro-Treaty members were asked to resign (they formed their own group, called Cumann na Saoirse (Society of Freedom), but were not militarily active). When O'Connell Street was evacuated, the women had tried to insist on staying with the rearguard, quoting the 1916 Proclamation which promised equal rights for women, but Brugha had eventually persuaded them to leave. C.S. Andrews later commented that the system of communications was the only really efficient part of the IRA operation during the war, thanks to the women.

Cumann na mBan played a larger role in the Civil War than in the War of Independence, and provided safe houses and medical care for the combatants. Women were useful as messengers, because they were less likely to be arrested and searched; at night, they would paint walls and pavements with slogans and news, evading censorship. Each branch had its own Intelligence Officer, and the women involved themselves in such activities as arranging funerals (including firing volleys over the grave), hunger-striking for prisoners' rights, and organising commemorations of the dead. Very few of them were active fighters, but as auxiliaries they were indispensable. At the end of the war they tried to assert their right to have a say in the ceasefire negotiations, but they were ignored.

Liam Lynch's policy seemed to be to fight a defensive war, retreating when attacked, but a few bold initiatives might have got better results. General O'Duffy, on the Free State side, was able to say: 'The enemy has already lost much by not taking the initiative and operating throughout the whole country while our strength was, more or less, dissipated in the capture of Dublin'. As Republican-held barracks were reached by Free State troops, the Republicans abandoned them one by one, and Lynch's headquarters moved from place to place without any logic or plan. O'Malley wrote to Lynch in July, 'Could you give me an outline of your Military and National policy as we are in the dark here with regard to both?'

Looting and commandeering of supplies made the Irregulars extremely unpopular. They were unable to keep prisoners, having barely enough food and accommodation for their own men, so had to let them go. Besides, they had their own political disagreements to deal with; some stood out for the full Republic, but others were ready to follow de Valera's idea of External Association. Local and personal rivalries also caused trouble among the officers, and military advantages were lost through lack of agreement on tactics. The military commanders would not allow political leaders such as Childers any military role, so they lost much useful

At Charleville I checked with the local commandant. He was still in bed but he assured me that there wasn't an enemy soldier within miles. What he failed to remember was that it was Sunday, and on Sunday the whole Irish race is unanimously moved to go to Mass, so that at that very moment our whole nine-mile front, pickets, machine-gun posts, fortresses and all, had simply melted away, and there wasn't as much as a fallen tree between me and the enemy. In itself that mightn't be too bad because it might also be assumed that there wouldn't be any enemy pickets either; but a considerable number of the enemy facing us were from the neighbourhood of Charleville, and after his longing for Mass, an Irishman's strongest characteristic is his longing for home and Mother, and anyone who knew his Ireland would have guessed that on that fine summer morning our whole front was being pierced in a dozen places by nostalgic enemy soldiers, alone or in force, all pining to embrace their mothers and discover if the cow had calved...

advice and assistance. They did not seem interested in setting up any kind of rival government or administration, and were apparently content just to fight, without any consideration of what future they were fighting for.

The Free State army was also in poor condition for war. Many of the soldiers had enlisted because of the pay, at a time of high unemployment, and officers complained frequently about the low standard of recruits and the lack of discipline, although the army also included many Irish ex-British Army veterans. At the start of the war, few of the troops were properly armed; as General MacMahon later recalled, 'men were taught the mechanism of a rifle very often on the way to a fight'.

Mulcahy was told by O'Duffy later, 'We had to get work out of a disgruntled, undisciplined and cowardly crowd. Arms were handed over wholesale to the enemy, sentries were drunk at their posts, and when a whole garrison was put in clink owing to insubordination, etc., the garrison sent to replace them often turned out to be worse'. Mulcahy himself later testified that a large proportion of 'the criminal element' existed in the army, and that experienced old soldiers were too often under the command of inexperienced officers, leading to lack of discipline.

Supplies were distributed inefficiently, and there were constant complaints about shortages of equipment, and about delays in payment. The Bank of Ireland, finally realising that the Provisional Government was the only likely defence against anarchy and was running the risk of bankruptcy, released funds after many requests, and two officers set off around the country to pay the troops in the nick of time.

Another problem for the government was prison accommodation. The prisons were quickly overcrowded, and it was difficult to get decent officers to run them. Sometimes Republican prisoners were released if they promised to stop fighting, but they usually went back to their units. Kilmainham was turned into a military prison, and Gormanstown Camp was used for internees. 12,000 prisoners were housed at the Curragh Camp. Rioting took place in Mountjoy prison, over the desperate conditions, and the Bishop of Limerick complained about conditions in Limerick prison.

Maud Gonne MacBride established the Women's Prisoners Defence League, which operated through the Civil War and after it. Known as 'The Mothers', the members of the league gathered every day outside prison gates, giving help and information to anxious relatives, and tracing missing men. They publicised the increasingly repressive treatment of prisoners, and held meetings in O'Connell Street every Sunday, to protest at the appalling prison conditions. They often found themselves driven off by water-hoses and even once by bullets.

As the war progressed, the Provisional Government became more ruthless in dealing with dissent. The Criminal Investigation Dept., run by Collins, contained a plain-clothes group of operatives called the 'Oriel House Gang', from their Dublin address. They were often accused of brutal treatment of prisoners and suspected spies, and a blind eye seems to have been turned to deaths in the course of 'interrogation'.

The government also suspended sittings of the Republican Supreme Court. They wished to take over the existing British court system instead, keeping it in operation until the whole system could be reorganised. The Republican courts, which had operated during the War of Independence, were now an embarrassment to the government, challenging many arrests as illegal. As an added confusion, people who

Union Quay in Cork City burning after the Republican retreat from Free State troops, who landed by sea. Photographed by Frank Brewitt, whose impressions are quoted on page 92 (National Archives of Ireland).

were not satisfied with a decision in one court would appeal to the rival system. These courts were finally abolished completely, and Gavan Duffy, Minister for Foreign Affairs, resigned on this issue.

The Course Of The War

Headlines taken from the *Freeman's Journal* will help here to give an idea of the course of events. However, it must be

---

Margaret Buckley's Hunger Strike

We had been refused the Sacraments. Only a week before I had tried to get Confession, but the priest, after arguing with me for an hour, did not hear my Confession. I told him I would likely be going on hunger strike, that I hoped I would die on it rather than give in, and that now I placed all my sins on him: I had done my part, and he had refused to do his, as ordained by God. I was rather sorry for him then. He was genuinely affected, and said 'Very well, child, I'll take the responsibility,' and left the box.

---

remembered that all news published about the war was heavily censored, and necessarily gave the Provisional Government point of view.

'HOW BLESSINGTON FELL.
'National troops' victorious advance on a twenty-mile front.
'OVER ONE HUNDRED
PRISONERS TAKEN.
'Rest of the Irregulars disperse into
mountainous district.' (10.7.22)

As the Irregulars evacuated Dublin, they fought Free State troops in the surrounding counties. Men from South Tipperary stationed themselves in Blessington, Co. Wicklow, hoping to attack Dublin, but the city was cordoned off by Free State troops and the republicans gradually dispersed; over 100 were arrested. Ernie O'Malley's forces captured several towns in County Wexford, but attempts to link up with other groups did not work out, and they had to evacuate. O'Malley returned to Dublin, receiving on the way a message from Lynch which appointed him Assistant Chief of Staff, and urged him to organize the provinces of Ulster and Leinster. 'All I could see was the futility of the order', said O'Malley.

News Brothers, Cork, to Easons, 19.8.22:
As far as the south of Ireland is concerned matters have become infinitely worse and as a result of the civil war we are entirely cut off from communications with the rest of the country and our customers generally. All railway and road bridges have been destroyed. Cork is now quite isolated and the Free State Army holding it is practically in a state of siege. Before evacuating the city last week the Republicans entered one of our offices and smashed machinery value £20,000 with sledge-hammers; similar outrages occurred in many places. Our business, except in the news departments is now entirely closed down as it is impossible to deliver goods or collect money, and we have no option therefore but to ask for a moratorium at present in regard to our debt to you.
From L.M. Cullen, *Eason & Son, A History*

North-east

'Dundalk barracks and full garrison captured
by national troops.
Great haul of Lewis and Thompson guns, ammunition and
bombs.' (17.7.22)
'DESCENT ON DUNDALK.
'Irregulars capture three barracks.
'BIG CASUALTIES.' (15.8.22)
'Recapture of Dundalk.
'Irregulars also retreat from Greenore and Carlingford.'
(18.8.22)

The recapture of Dundalk on 14 August was a great morale-booster for the Irregulars. Frank Aiken, in charge of the area, had wanted to remain neutral, and stayed in contact with Mulcahy until he was arrested in July. Escaping from prison, he helped in the recapture of Dundalk, and when the Free State troops recovered it his troops dispersed to the mountains.

South-east

'WATERFORD CITY TAKEN.
'River Suir Crossed At Night.'(21.7.22)
'Irregulars preparing to make a stand
at Carrick-on-Suir.'(26.7.22)
'Irregulars evacuate Callan before National Forces arrive.
'COUNTY KILKENNY CLEARANCE.
'Four hours' fight in open country near Bailieboro.' 12.8.22)
'CARRICK-ON-SUIR TAKEN.
'300 Irregulars retire after destroying bridges.
'Clonmel rendered untenable by the recent advances.' (4.8.22)

The taking of Waterford, which was surrounded by Republican areas, gave the Free State troops a strong tactical advantage. Tensions and disputes among the Irregular leaders there meant that the city was surrendered quite quickly, and support, which had been expected from Cork and Tipperary, was inadequate. In the Tipperary area, the Irregular commanders acted individually, and their failure to co-operate meant that isolated groups could be easily overcome.

South/South-west

(22.7.22) 'FALL OF LIMERICK.
'Powerful night assault compels the Irregulars to retreat.'
'Many mines on the roads to Cork.' (1.8.22)
'FIGHTING AT BRUREE.
'9 Irregulars die in County Limerick.
'Attackers pursued to Kilmallock.' (4.8.22)
'MARCH INTO COUNTY KERRY.
'The capture of Tralee.
'Tarbert and Ballylongford taken:
advance on Listowel.' (5.8.22)

'Blessing the Colours' – painting by Sir John Lavery (Hugh Lane Municipal Gallery, Dublin) – a tribute to the honour and pride of the new state and its army.

'The Funeral of Harry Boland' by Jack Yeats (Sligo Museum and Library) – an artist's tribute to the admired Republican.

'Arthur Griffith' by Sir John Lavery (Hugh Lane Municipal Gallery, Dublin) – the founder in 1904 of Sinn Féin, was a constititutionalist rather than a revolutionary Republican, whose health broke down under the pressure of events in 1922.

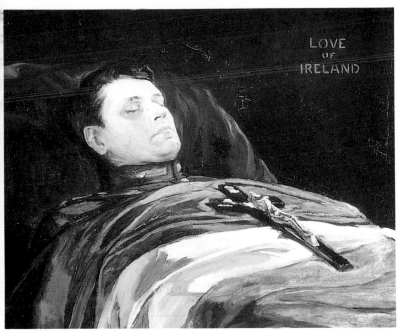

'Love of Ireland (Collins lying in state)' by Sir John Lavery – the shock of Collins' death affected all Irish people. **Below:** The shared vision of both sides in the Civil War: a rural, Catholic, traditional Ireland, epitomised in this 1929 painting of pilgrims – 'St Patrick's Purgatory' by Sir John Lavery (Hugh Lane Municipal Gallery, Dublin).

'Communicating with the Prisoners' by Jack Yeats (Sligo Museum and Library) – friends calling up to the women prisoners in Kilmainham Gaol.

Top: 'Kevin O'Higgins' (Hugh Lane Municipal Gallery, Dublin) — held responsible by Republicans for the December 1922 reprisal executions, murdered 10 July 1927: according to Yeats a man incapable of remorse or regret.

Bottom: Ballyseedy memorial to the murdered IRA volunteers in Co. Kerry, by Breton sculptor Yann Renard-Goullet (Photo: Michael Diggin, Tralee).

Pádraig Ó Buacalla   Pádraig Ó haimtnéada
Seán Ó Concubair   Tadg Ó Tuama
Seán Ó dálaig   Seoirse Ó Séagda
Séamus breatnac   micheál Ó Conaill

Ar deis Dé go raib a n-ainmneaca

FROM THIS DAY FORTH ALL WHO PASS THIS WAY WILL KNOW THAT THE MEN OF KERRY WHO FOUGHT AND DIED FOR IRELAND ARE NOT FORGOTTEN AND THEIR MEMORY WILL ENDURE AS LONG AS THIS BRONZE MEMORIAL STANDS AT BALLYSEEDY

UNSELFISH UPHOLDERS AND FEARLESS DEFENDERS OF THE IRISH REPUBLIC THESE EIGHT MEN OF KERRY WHOSE NAMES WE TRACE WITH PRIDE AND REMEMBER WITH HOMAGE SUFFERED MARTYRDOM ON THIS SPOT ON THE NIGHT OF MARCH 6TH – 7TH 1923

THIS MEMORIAL ALSO COMMEMORATES THEIR COMRADES
DENIS BRODERICK
JOHN CALVIN
MICHAEL RYLE
SEAMUS TAYLOR
WHO DIED FOR IRELAND IN THIS LOCALITY

*'Coalisland and Farranfore taken by army
in County Kerry.' (9.8.22)*
*'NATIONAL FORCES LAND AT THREE POINTS ON
CORK COAST.*
*'National army now in control in Abbeyfeale and
Drumcollogher.' (10.8.22)*
'IRREGULARS APPLY TORCH TO CORK.
'National troops at the gates.' (11.8.22)
'Mallow, Fermoy and Mitchelstown captured by the army.
*'People keep constant vigil on bridge
to prevent destruction.' (17.8.22)*

The struggle for Limerick was a turning-point in the Civil War. The Republican forces held most of the Limerick barracks at the start, with at least 700 troops. Lynch set up his HQ there, and engaged in truce talks with Michael Brennan, commander of the Free State army in the area, but O'Duffy soon stopped this. He had heard that Brennan was anxious for an agreement, and was afraid he would resign his command, taking most of his troops with him. However, a truce agreement was reached on 7 July.

Brennan said he agreed to this to prevent the Irregulars marching on Dublin. Lynch felt that the truce would help him to consolidate Republican control of Munster, but most of his officers were annoyed by the truce, wanting a more aggressive policy. Free State reinforcements began to arrive, and the Limerick truce was later seen as demoralising to the Irregulars.

The Provisional Government, breaking the truce, attacked Limerick and won it after two days of fierce fighting and destruction in the city centre. The Republican troops managed to escape, and the fight moved on to the surrounding counties. The fighting at Kilmallock was one of the few 'proper' battles in the Civil War.

The technique of landing at sea, Emmet Dalton's idea, was a great success at Cork, and the Irregulars evacuated the city without a fight. They had censored the local press, seized goods and money, and brought the local economy to a standstill; the Free State troops were a welcome sight to most of the citizens. The Irregulars moved into the county and continued the fight, but their troops were disorganised, and the leadership in disagreement.

The guerrilla war was fought most fiercely in Kerry, an area where the Free State troops found it very difficult to make headway. However, despite advance warnings the Irregulars failed to defend Kerry against sea landings, and were driven out of Fenit, Tarbert, Listowel and Kenmare. They still held some towns, and continued a very vigorous programme of ambushes and flying column attacks; they had a lot of support from the local population, and maintained a strong resistance to the end.

In the fighting all over Ireland, the civilians suffered as much as the combatants (Cashman Collection RTE)

West

'MAYO'S TIME OF TRIAL.
'Effects of Irregular occupation.
'Ruined homes: arrests: aged people starving.'(20.7.22)
'Ballyhaunis taken.
'Castlerea welcomes the national troops.
'PEACE IN SLIGO.' (24.7.22)
'Fall of Westport secured by landing from the sea.
'All the towns of Connacht cleared of the Irregulars.
'Ballaghadereen Evacuated.' (8.7.22)
'IRREGULARS IN FLIGHT.
'Positions abandoned after a three hours' battle in Mayo.
'NATIONAL FORCES SURROUND AND CAPTURE
IRREGULARS IN COUNTY GALWAY.' (10.8.22)

In the west most of the IRA were anti-Treaty, but were moving in scattered, isolated groups, out of touch with the main events. When the Free State troops landed in Westport by sea, they took over the surrounding area without much difficulty. The Irregulars headed for the mountains.

Donegal

(17.7.22) 'Island fortress falls.
'Irregulars' stronghold in Donegal captured by the troops.'

Donegal contained large numbers of Irregulars at the start of the war, including troops of the 1st Southern Division, but they were isolated and living in poor conditions, as reported by Charlie Daly, their commander: 'The country is so assuredly poor that we could hardly get enough to eat. We were often glad when we could get potatoes and salt, or a bit of bread and a drop of tea...' Ernie O'Malley finally ordered the abandonment of Donegal in November 1922, as he felt the men would be more useful elsewhere. Daly had been captured, and was executed with three other Irregulars in March 1923.

23.8.22

3.15 a.m.

To the men
of the Army —

Stand calmly by your posts.

Bend bravely and undaunted to
your work

Let no cruel act of reprisal
blemish your bright honour.

Every dark hour that Michael
Collins met since 1916 served but
to steel that bright strength of his
and temper his gay bravery

You are left each inheritors of
that strength, and of that bravery

To each of you falls his
unfinished work.

No darkness in the hour —
no loss of comrade will daunt
you at it

Ireland ! The Army serves —
strengthened by its sorrow.

Risteárd Ua Maolchatha
Chief of the General Staff

General Mulcahy's message to the new National Army after the death of General
Collins (From The Voice of Ireland, courtesy Central Catholic Library)

CHAPTER 5

The Toll of Death

On 12 August 1922, Arthur Griffith died from a cerebral haemorrhage, having been ill for some time. He was only fifty-one years old, but had been carrying a very heavy burden of responsibility. Sean MacEoin said of him, 'Griffith sacrificed his life – a life of great ability – for the Irish people. He was the poorest man in Ireland when he died'. De Valera wrote, 'He was, I believe, unselfishly patriotic and courageously'.

At Griffith's graveside Michael Collins said, 'In memory of Arthur Griffith let us resolve now to give fresh play to the impulse of unity, to join together one and all in continuing his constructive work, in building up the country which he loved'. William Cosgrave, a Sinn Féin TD since 1917, and Minister for Local Government, now became Acting President of the Dáil.

Collins had broken off a tour of southern barracks to attend the funeral, and he resumed this tour on 20 August, disregarding warnings that it was not safe. He was certainly undertaking a tour of inspection, and was also hoping to get back some of the money which Irregulars had commandeered in local bank raids. However, it is possible that he was also hoping to meet some of the Irregular leaders, using his old IRB contacts, and to halt the Civil War in some way.

Above: August 1922: The State Funeral of Arthur Griffith, President of the Executive Council of the Irish Free State. General Mulcahy (first right) and Michael Collins (third right) outside Dublin Pro-Cathedral (Courtesy Central Catholic Library) **Below**: Griffith funeral passes Oriel House, notorious headquarters of the special police, where Republican prisoners were said to have been ill-treated (Murtagh Collection RTE)

> **'Your hour has come'**
> ...Children were playing an exciting game. Placing a board on little wheels to represent a motor-lorry, they invited one of their number to mount the board, while another drove it along, till, as he approached a corner, he said with due solemnity, 'Your hour has come!' and turned the car into the very arms of another group who proceeded with the assassination in due form...
> Henry Nevinson, *Last Changes, Last Chances*

He was taking a great risk in travelling around some of the most dangerous parts of the country with only a small escort, and it would not have needed the Commander-in-Chief himself to inspect a collection of barracks. He had not been well and seemed depressed, but would not be put off going, saying that his own people (of Co. Cork, where he had been born) would not kill him.

On 22 August Collins left Cork city with Emmet Dalton and a small escort. They passed through Béal na mBláth, an isolated valley, on the way to Bandon, and a group of Irregulars laid an ambush, expecting them to return the same way. (In nearby Ballyvourney, two days before, de Valera and

Poor children selling apples at Collins funeral: symptoms of the real social problems of the new Ireland (Cashman Collection RTE)

The new unarmed Civic Guards take over Dublin Castle, August 1922 (Cashman Collection RTE)

other Irregulars had been holding a staff meeting in the same area, but this seems to have been only a coincidence.) When by 8 o'clock that night no-one had passed, most of the ambushers retired to a nearby pub.

Five men were left to clear the barricade, and suddenly heard Collins's group approaching and took cover. When they fired on the convoy, Dalton ordered the men to drive on, but Collins countermanded him, and a short battle took place. As the attackers retreated Collins was found lying on the ground, with a gaping hole in his neck. While Dalton tried to bandage it, Michael Collins died.

Republicans in action in the south of Ireland, a posed picture for propaganda purposes (at which Erskine Childers was a master) (From The Voice of Ireland, courtesy Central Catholic Library)

Above: Train wrecked near Cloughjordan, Co. Tipperary, by Republicans (Courtesy Sean Sexton Historical Collection)
Below: Repairing Mallow bridge, blown up by Republicans, an outrage Childers was alleged to have master-minded (Cashman Collection RTE)

The news spread swiftly round the country, and was greeted with shock and disbelief; he had seemed indestructible. Tom Barry received the news in Kilmainham jail: 'I looked down on the extraordinary spectacle of about a thousand kneeling Republican prisoners spontaneously reciting the Rosary aloud for the repose of the soul of the dead Michael Collins...'

The death of Collins, the most charismatic leader in the Provisional Government, could have led to a major crisis. Many Republican leaders saw his death as an opportunity to press an offensive, but Mulcahy quickly reassured the Free State forces, and Cosgrave took over his role as Chairman of the Provisional Government, with the assistance of Kevin O'Higgins, Minister of Economic Affairs. Mulcahy now became Commander-in-Chief and Minister for Defence.

Cosgrave's statement on Collins's death ended: 'His death has sealed his work, and before the tragedy of his death the nation is resolved to bring the work to triumph'. In a tribute to both Griffith and Collins, Winston Churchill said they 'feared God, loved their country, and kept their word'. Collins's death led to a toughening on the Free State side, and some bitter army reprisals occurred despite Mulcahy's plea for restraint. The situation was even more unstable than before, and the government ministers, with their families, moved into Government Buildings in Merrion Street for protection. They lived there for months, under cramped and uncomfortable conditions, as they continued to establish the new administration.

During August 1922 Ernest Blythe, the only Ulster Protestant in the Provisional Government, wrote a memorandum on the Northern situation for his colleagues. He recommended that they must 'prepare the way for a state of feeling which may lead now or in the long run to the unity of Ireland', and stop harassing the Northern state. He knew

Literary links with the Civil War

It is significant that for many Irish writers it was the Civil War, with Irishman against Irishman, rather than the earlier War of Independence, that produced their best work.

Sean O'Casey's drama of the Civil War, *Juno and the Paycock* (1924) is regarded by many as his finest play. Liam O'Flaherty (who had fought on the Republican side in July 1922) used the Civil War and its sinister aftermath in many novels and short stories, including his most famous work *The Informer* (1925), a book which still touches a raw nerve in Irish society.

Younger writers, too, like Francis Stuart, Peadar O'Donnell, Frank O'Connor and Sean O'Faolain also fought with the Republicans.

W.B. Yeats, who was awarded the Nobel Prize for Literature in 1923, was also deeply affected by the events of the Civil War, and wrote a linked series of poems, *Meditations in Time of Civil War*, which reflect upon incidents he himself witnessed while living at Thoor Ballylee in Galway. Yeats was also a Free State Senator, and his house in Merrion Square was fired into by Republicans.

The poet's brother, the painter Jack Yeats, whose sympathies were with the Republicans, painted several incidents of the Civil War which moved him deeply (see colour illustrations).

These paintings, plays, poems and stories retain the bitter experience of a testing time for later generations.

that they would be accused of deserting Northern National-ists, but the policy of destabilisation could not work, and the only chance of unity left was to end unnecessary irritations. Nationalist MPs should be encouraged to take their seats in the Northern Parliament, the payment of Northern teachers should end, and border incidents should be prevented.

From now on, the Northern Nationalists would be on their own; Collins had been the driving force behind much of the Free State's Northern policy, and now he was gone. Their isolation was made worse by legislation passed in Northern Ireland in September, which abolished propor-tional representation for local elections and imposed an oath

IRA unit in action in Sligo during the last days of the Civil War (Belfast Telegraph)

Artillery Officer (after fruitless attempts to shell sniper out of tree): " Say, Seán, skip down to the village and get a saw."

of allegiance on all members of local authorities. The number of Nationalist-controlled councils was gradually reduced by half.

The Third Dáil met on 5 September. Republican members abstained from attending, so the only opposition was provided by the Labour Party. The Second Dáil was finally officially wound up, but not in the eyes of the anti-Treaty TDs; they considered that they still embodied it. The new cabinet was headed by William Cosgrave as President and Minister for Finance, and included Desmond Fitzgerald, Ernest Blythe, Patrick Hogan, Joseph McGrath, J.J. Walsh, Eoin MacNeill, Kevin O'Higgins and Richard Mulcahy. This cabinet contained every member of the original Provisional Government still living, and made no reference at all to the pre-election Coalition Pact. The Governor-General was to be T.M. Healy; related to Kevin O'Higgins by marriage, he had been a member of the old Irish Parliamentary Party during the 1880s, and had been a leader of the group which brought about Parnell's downfall.

Thirty nominations to the Senate included sixteen Southern Unionists, as well as prominent Nationalists such as W.B. Yeats and Oliver St John Gogarty, and another thirty Senators were chosen by the Dáil through proportional representation. The Senate, although it had limited powers, proved to be of great value to the Free State, demonstrating that Nationalists and Unionists could work together for the good of the country. Thirty-six of its members were Catholic, and 24 non-Catholic.

The first business at hand was to pass the new Constitution. This was followed by a Public Safety Bill, introduced on 27 September, which set up military courts. These courts could impose the death penalty on anyone found carrying arms or ammunition, or who committed any act of war; prisoners would no longer be treated as political prisoners. Severe censorship was imposed on the media. The executions which resulted from the use of these courts (seventy-seven executions by the end of the war) provoked further reprisals from the Irregulars. The prospect of official executions caused great unease in the Free State army; it had been difficult enough to get soldiers to fight against ex-comrades and old friends. On 3 October, a government proclamation offered an amnesty to surrendering Irregulars, but the response was very small.

The Catholic bishops issued a joint pastoral in October, supporting the Free State. They described the anti-Treaty forces as carrying on 'what they call a war, but which, in the absence of any legitimate authority to justify it, is morally only a system of murder...' The pastoral had little effect on the Irregulars, however, who saw it only as a betrayal of the Republic. As Peadar O'Donnell said later, 'Generations of pious thought had hallowed the old greeting among women, "May you be the mother of a bishop", but in the jails of 1922 Irish girls hurled it at one another as a malediction.'

Meanwhile, the anti-Treaty fighters were becoming aware that they needed to have some kind of government of their own, and to develop political and social policies; Mellows pressed for a revival of the Democratic Programme of Sinn Féin. Lynch reluctantly agreed to an Army Executive meeting in October, and a Republican government was formed with de Valera as President. It could not, of course, function in any way, and several of its cabinet members, including Mellows, were in prison.

Executions

The first executions under the new legislation, of four men who had been captured with weapons, took place in November. These were followed on 24 November by the execution of Erskine Childers, one of the most important captures from the anti-Treaty side. In charge of Irregular propaganda, he was regarded by the Free State government as one of their most powerful enemies, and had been demonised, as can be seen in this *Freeman's Journal* editorial (18.8.22):

'...English fanatics like Mr Erskine Childers will urge them [the Irregulars] on to burn, wreck and destroy.

'Mr Childers had scruples, which Irishmen respected, about shooting his own countrymen in the Anglo-Irish War.

'He has none at all about killing Irish soldiers, and compassing the ruin of Irish voters who had the audacity to reject him at the polls.

'Do Irregulars really relish their position as the military puppets of this English ex-intelligence officer?'

Childers was charged with possessing a weapon (a small revolver Michael Collins had given him in friendship), and executed on the flimsiest of evidence, before a judicial appeal could be heard. The executions had already been having a negative effect on the public, and people were deeply upset by the ruthlessness of this episode.

The Irregulars responded to these executions with an attack on two TDs, Seán Hales and Padraic O Máille, on 7 December, during which Hales was killed. The following morning, four prisoners were taken from Mountjoy Jail and executed. These were Rory O'Connor, Liam Mellows, Joe McKelvey and Dick Barrett, and their executions were authorised by the Cabinet as a warning that government must not be attacked. The prisoners had not been tried in a court of law, and the executions horrified public opinion in both England and Ireland, not least because Kevin O'Higgins had been best man at O'Connor's wedding less than a year before.

The executions of these four men had the desired effect. Republican morale had been badly shaken, and TDs were no longer targeted, apart from an attack on Sean McGarry, TD, on 10 December; his house was burnt down and one of his children died. Families of TDs suffered as well; Kevin O'Higgins's father was killed in February 1923, Cosgrave's uncle was shot dead, and Cosgrave's home was burnt down.

Senators were targeted instead, mainly the Southern

Above: Symbolic funeral of Rory O'Connor staged by Sinn Féin women December 1922 (Illustrated London News) *Below*: The last Republican volunteer to die, James Quirke of Co. Limerick, lying in state. (Courtesy Sean Sexton Historical Collection)

The burning of Kilteragh, the home of Sir Horace Plunkett, creator of the Co-Operative movement, victim of the Republican campaign against the homes of senators (from The Voice of Ireland, courtesy Central Catholic Library)
The establishment of constitutionalism: In January 1923 President Cosgrave and his cabinet begin the work of creating the new state (From The Voice of Ireland, courtesy Central Catholic Library)

Unionist landowners. Many great houses were burnt down, thirty-seven between January and February 1923. Losses included Moore Hall, in Co. Mayo, and Oliver St John Gogarty's house at Renvyle, in Connemara. Kilteragh, the home of Horace Plunkett, a founder of the co-operative movement, was also burnt down, being attacked twice. Plunkett was away, and his secretary had to take defensive measures: 'I...got a builder to come out and begin to board up some of the windows, for people were hanging about to loot the place, and already a respectable-looking woman had driven over in a pony trap and had begun to dig up the rose trees in the front beds...'

The 'big house' attacks were largely motivated by destruction for its own sake – Horace Plunkett, for example, was a benefactor to Irish agriculture rather than an 'oppressor'. Large numbers of irreplaceable art treasures were lost (although rumours abound that unexpected glories lurked for years in isolated cottages). Lady Fingall recounts the saving, at the last moment, of Castletown House, in Co. Kildare: '...a breathless young man, with some mysterious authority, rode into the middle of the group of burners, to say that on no account was the house to be touched that had been built with Irish money by William Conolly, who was Speaker of the Irish House of Commons two hundred years or so earlier...'

Another tactic of the Irregulars was to destroy communications, and a programme of destruction was aimed at the railway network: 'a hundred bridges blown up are just as effective a blow...as a hundred barracks blown up'. Isolated rural areas found themselves cut off completely from other centres of population, and trade and agriculture were badly affected.

A Railroad Protection and Maintenance Corps was formed urgently, and was successful in its efforts to keep most lines open, despite the difficulties of getting equipment and supplies. So-called 'Tenants' Associations' were seizing land and cattle from their owners, using tactics of murder and arson; a sense of anarchy was spreading.

Government control tightened still further. The Criminal Investigation Department had been brought under central control after Collins's death, and was now helping to collect intelligence and to protect the homes of government ministers. Prisoners were interrogated for information, and spies were inserted into Republican units. Other activities also continued; Noel Lemass (brother of Sean), who had been suspected of involvement in the Seán Hayes murder, was captured in July 1923, and his body was found three months later in the Dublin mountains. It was widely believed that the CID were responsible.

In February 1923 the Free State army was reorganised, and many of the over-large commands were split up, but it was still not fully professional. In March, a Supreme War Council was set up; it had a civilian majority, and had powers to recommend the removal of officers, and to supervise strategy. Mulcahy was furious, seeing this as an undermining of his authority, and resigned immediately from the Army Council, but Cosgrave persuaded him to cancel his resignation.

The government established a policy of holding prisoners as 'hostages'; executions were cancelled if the areas the prisoners came from stopped fighting. This placed further strain on the Irregulars, who were already short of food and equipment, isolated and low in morale. They were living off the country, which mostly did not want to have them, and for most of them the future was bleak. Reminiscences dwell on the discomfort of lice ('their numbers and size...were phenomenal'), the constant movement from one safe house to another, and the terror of hidden men as bales of hay were poked and prodded with bayonets.

The war dragged on, however, because there seemed to

be no way out. The Irregulars would never recognise the Free State government and give up the dream of a Republic. It was Liam Lynch, in fact, who almost single-handed kept them fighting long past the time when it made any sense. The capture of Liam Deasy, a Cork leader, in January 1923 was a heavy blow. Deasy agreed to issue a letter which said: 'I accept and I will aid in immediate and unconditional surrender of arms and men as required by General Mulcahy', because he had decided that honourable retreat would help to conserve Republican ideals, and that there was little point in fighting on.

Michael Brennan later said that this was 'the greatest act of moral courage I have known in my life'. Deasy's appeal was very effective among the thousands of prisoners who had little hope of a successful conclusion, despite the reaction of Ernie O'Malley: 'The chaplain...hinted that I should follow Deasy's example...I am glad I got to contain myself when he was in my cell, but when he left I went up in smoke'.

The anti-Treaty leaders held a four-day Executive meeting in March, in Co. Kilkenny, but they could not agree on a policy; they would meet again three weeks later, they decided. However, they had taken a great risk in coming together, and in fact several of them, including Austin Stack and Dan Breen, were arrested as they tried to rejoin their units. The greatest Irregular loss, however, was the Commander-in-Chief, Liam Lynch, who was shot and killed on 10 April while trying to escape Free State troops in the Knockmealdown mountains, Co. Tipperary.

To the last stages of the Civil War belong some of the worst atrocities.

In Knocknagoshel, Co. Kerry, on 6 March, five Free State soldiers were killed by a mine, so Paddy Daly, Free State commander in the area, announced that Republican prisoners were to be used to clear mines in future. On 7 March nine prisoners were marched to Ballyseedy Cross, near Tralee, and eight were blown up there by a mine. According to the account of the survivor, Stephen Fuller, who was blown clear, the prisoners had been tied together around the mine, which was then deliberately detonated. The troops collecting the fragments of bodies from trees and bushes did not realise that one prisoner was not accounted for. There was almost a riot in Tralee when relatives insisted on opening the coffins.

The following day four more prisoners were killed by a mine at Countess Bridge, near Killarney, and on 12 March five were blown up at Cahirciveen; it was said that they had first been shot in the legs, to prevent escape. These were all deliberate killings, of prisoners who had not been tried, and their memory has blackened the reputation of the Free State army ever since.

CHAPTER 6

Conclusion

By the early months of 1923, it was obvious that the Irregular campaign was weakening. However, their propaganda continued untiringly, mainly owning to the efforts of Cumann na mBan. Countess Markievicz was touring Scotland and England, addressing public meetings and Sinn Féin clubs, calling for support. *Poblacht na hEireann*, now called *Eire, The Irish Nation*, worked against the slant of the heavily-censored main national newspapers (Ernie O'Malley was not impressed by it: 'The tone adopted was one such as if we were all the spoiled darlings of the nation, the majority of whom followed with interest our every action. Total lack of dignity and truth seemed to me to sum up our propaganda'). But the end was in sight.

In Cork, Republicans had been driven into the mountains, and more than 5,000 Free State troops were in command of the city. Republican morale remained strong, however, in parts of Kerry, and was helped by the brutal behaviour of the Free State forces in this county, such as the Ballyseedy atrocity; as the Free State commander, Paddy Daly, said: 'No-one told me to bring kid gloves, so I didn't'. Clearing of Irregular forces in the West took place after the Free State consolidated its control of Munster. However, Sligo railway station was burnt down by an IRA party, and Ballyconnell,

Co. Sligo, was raided, and in both cases the Free State response was late and ineffective. It was suspected that some government troops were still sympathetic to the Republican cause.

In Dublin, in March 1923, the Irregulars ordered a ban on all public amusements, but the government put pressure on theatres and cinemas to stay open. An international boxing match planned for St Patrick's Night was not included in the ban; presumably it was felt there was a limit to what the sporting public would bear. In the North, military activity had almost completely ended; it seemed the Republicans were leaving that business aside, until the Boundary Commission had done its work. The northern government was taking advantage of the southern Civil War to clamp down on the IRA and the Nationalist population; the new Unionist state was able to consolidate itself without meeting any serious resistance.

Ceasefire

In April 1923 Monsignor Luzio arrived in Ireland, sent by the Vatican as a peace envoy in response to Republican requests. However, the Provisional Government insisted on treating his visit merely as a matter of courtesy, and would not discuss the war with him; he was recalled to Rome without achieving anything. Still seeking a resolution to their difficulties, the Army Executive of the IRA met on 20 April, and elected Frank Aiken as Chief of Staff in succession to Lynch. They discussed proposals for peace, but could not agree. However, a later meeting with de Valera and the Republican government authorised Aiken to issue a 'Suspension of Offensive' order, to arrange a truce.

De Valera issued a Proclamation giving the terms on which peace could be negotiated, and senators Andrew Jameson and James Douglas acted as intermediaries.

However, the terms proposed were impossible for the government to agree to. The Oath was to be removed, IRA funding and property was to be restored, and one demand was for buildings where the IRA could store their arms under seal. O'Higgins retorted: 'This is not going to be a draw, with a replay in the autumn.' Contacts continued for some time without success.

Finally, the Irregulars decided simply to dump arms, and the order was issued by Aiken on 24 May 1923. De Valera followed with another proclamation, praising the IRA: 'Military victory must be allowed to rest for the moment with those who have destroyed the Republic...You have saved the nation's honour, preserved the sacred national tradition, and kept open the road of independence'. The order to dump arms was obeyed, except in isolated instances; most of the fighting had ended already, and hundreds of fighters had simply headed for their homes. However, Free State troops continued for some time to search for arms, and to make arrests.

De Valera wanted to keep the idea of the Republic alive, and argued that anti-Treaty candidates should fight in the August 1923 election which was to end the Provisional Government, and set up the Free State officially. Their original policy had been not to recognise the existence of the Free State at all, but he said: 'The more progress we make at the coming elections, the more certain will be our victory at the subsequent elections. The elections give an opportunity for

Dramatic artist's impression of the arrest of de Valera by Free State troops while speaking at Ennis, August 1923: effectively the end of the Civil War (Illustrated London News)

explaining our position and reaching the people, which I think should be availed of'.

De Valera was more or less on the run by now, and was finally arrested by Free State troops when he spoke at an election meeting in Ennis (although he won the seat). Seats were also won by Countess Markievicz, Mary MacSwiney and Austin Stack, but when the votes were finally counted, the Free State party (now called Cumann na Gaedheal) had won 64 seats to the Republicans' 44. The Republican vote was, however, larger than expected; there was still a lot of Republican support around the country, and many otherwise non-Republican voters had been alienated by the government's tactics during the Civil War. Sinn Féin complained of intimidation by government forces during the campaign.

William Cosgrave remained President of the Executive Council (until 1932) and Mulcahy as Minister of Defence; Blythe became Minister for Finance, and Kevin O'Higgins Minister of Home Affairs. The Labour Party dropped from 17 seats to 14. The only woman elected who actually took her seat in the new Dáil was Margaret Collins O'Driscoll, a sister of Michael Collins. The Irish Free State now applied to the League of Nations, not as a Dominion but as 'Saorstát Eireann', and was admitted as a member on 10 September.

De Valera was in prison for a year, in Kilmainham and in Arbour Hill, and used the time to consolidate his position as President of the phantom Republican government. He could not, however, overcome the abstention policy, which meant that there was no Republican voice in the Dáil. It was to be 1927 before he founded a new party, Fianna Fáil, and entered the Dáil, breaking completely with Sinn Féin. He had been forced into this action after the assassination of Kevin O'Higgins in July 1927. In response to this murder, an Electoral Amendment act required every intending Dáil candidate to swear an affidavit that they would sign the Oath and take their seat if elected; abstention was no longer an option.

De Valera signed the book containing the Oath, calling it an 'empty formula', but declared that he had not taken the Oath. As far as the Free State government was concerned, he might as well have done this much in 1922. Indeed, when he finally came to power as Taoiseach in 1932, he admitted surprise at finding how much independence the Treaty had actually given the Free State.

Aftermath

There had not been a proper negotiated ceasefire, so there were none of the usual official signs a war had ended. Prisoners were released slowly and gradually, and the strict public safety laws were kept in place. The new unarmed Civic Guard, under Eoin O'Duffy, had great difficulty in establishing its authority in disaffected areas; land theft by random armed groups was still a problem, and administration such as the collection of income tax was in tatters.

In June 1923 a Public Order Bill, which the Labour Party opposed, established powers of internment, and penalties such as flogging for arson and robbery. There were complaints in the Dáil against continuing a policy of repression, and opinion against the government hardened. Large numbers of prisoners were still being held in appallingly overcrowded conditions.

One of the worst manifestations of prison violence took place in April 1923, when women prisoners, including Mary MacSwiney and Kate O'Callaghan, went on hunger strike in Kilmainham and Mountjoy. A letter from one of the other women describes Mrs O'Callaghan and Madame MacBride as 'very much wasted...Mary MacS. is the same grand spirit but ever so much weaker this time on her 12th day...' The women were informed they would be moved to the North Dublin Union, an old workhouse which had been converted to a jail, and they decided to resist forcibly.

Free State troops and police engaged them in a brutal struggle for five hours, and several women were seriously hurt before they were finally removed to the NDU: '...Mrs Gordon...clung to the iron bars, the men beat her hands with their clenched fists again and again; that failed to make her loose her hold, and they struck her twice in the chest, then one took her head and beat it against the iron bars...'(Dorothy MacArdle). Mrs O'Callaghan and Mary MacSwiney were released the following day.

Maud Gonne MacBride's WPDL continued its work, keeping the question of prisoners before the public eye. The slow rate of releases helped tensions to build, and led to a mass hunger-strike, beginning on 13 October 1923. It was claimed that over 8,000 prisoners took part; certainly many started on the strike who would not have been allowed to do so if the Republican leadership had had any real control over the situation.

Hundreds refused food, instead of a few hand-picked men and women with the health and the will to continue for any length of time. It was a kind of mass movement, without any clear purpose or demand, and ended in many prisons after about three weeks. It was finally called off towards the end of November, but not before two men had died. The general result was demoralising for the Republican side. The government gradually released larger numbers of prisoners, and all Civil War prisoners had been freed by mid-1924.

The Free State still had to cope with continuing labour unrest. Agricultural labourers went on strike in the spring of 1923, and in July, after dockers' daily rates were reduced by employers, a dock strike paralysed the economy for months. The labour movement was riven with rivalries and dissensions, and was continually attacked both by Sinn Féin, who saw it as a lackey of the government, and by Cumann na nGaedheal, who accused it of contributing to civil unrest. Cosgrave would not negotiate, and the wave of strikes gradually collapsed. Membership of the Irish Congress of Trade Unions dropped, from 175,000 in 1924 to 92,000 by 1929; the labour movement had been sidelined by the Civil War, and took years to recover.

Rural unrest was calmed by Patrick Hogan, Minister for Agriculture, whose Land Act in late 1923 completed land reforms which the British had begun years before. The state was given power to acquire land compulsorily in order to distribute it to tenants, and landowners would be compensated in bonds backed by the British and Irish governments. Culture was not neglected either; film censorship was introduced in 1923, and the *Cork Weekly Examiner* asserted that one of the biggest problems facing the government was the training of thousands of school-teachers to give instruction in the Irish language, now compulsory in schools.

Now fighting had ended, the Free State Army at 50,000 strong was far too large and expensive for the country in peacetime, and needed to be reduced to about 20,000 troops. Discipline in the army was still poor, and some officers and men were being accused by the public of crimes such as theft and assault. The demobilisations caused severe problems, with men refusing to lay down their arms or to leave their barracks, and of course contributed even further to an already high level of unemployment. A resettlement bureau tried to help officers who were surplus to requirements to return to civilian life.

Unrest within the officer corps was brought to a head by divisions between the so-called 'Old IRA' (a group led by members of Collins's old intelligence unit), and Minister for Defence Mulcahy; they felt he had excluded them from the IRB after Collins's death. Joe McGrath, Minister for Industry and Commerce, was their voice in the government. In March 1924 an ultimatum from these disaffected officers demanded the removal of the Army Council, and an end to demobilisations. They were worried that the government seemed to be content that the Free State was the end for which the Treaty had been signed, not the means to that end.

O'Higgins refused to be intimidated; forty officers resigned, and more absconded with war materials. McGrath resigned from the government, and Eoin O'Duffy was put in charge of the army. Mulcahy had to resign as Minister for Defence, because O'Higgins suspected him of seeking a military dictatorship. The Army Council was dismissed. A report on the 'mutiny', issued in June, saw Mulcahy as simply a victim of the affair. This was the end of the IRB within the army; all soldiers now had to take an oath that they did not belong to any secret society. The army had become fully an instrument of the government, not the other way round.

Boundary Commission

The Boundary Commission was not brought into being until 1924. Its functions were unclear, and one member refused to co-operate; Sir James Craig would not nominate a Northern Ireland commissioner. It was important to the British that the Boundary Commission should go ahead, because it had been part of the Treaty and one of the main reasons the Irish delegates had signed it at all, so they appointed J.R. Fisher to fill the gap, a friend of Craig's who had already been urging him to hold on to Donegal. Eoin MacNeill, who was from County Antrim, was the Free State nominee; one of his sons had died on the Republican side during the Civil War. The official British commissioner was Mr Justice Richard Feetham, of the South African Supreme Court.

The Free State government was nervous about the negotiations; Ireland and Britain were still closely linked in terms of economy and trade, and Britain owed Ireland no favours. As Cosgrave admitted, 'Every step we take to improve our own position must, in the beginning at least, limit the profits hitherto earned in Ireland on sales and purchases by Britishers. In consequence we lose politically, and when such losses are sustained here by our own citizens there is also a lessening of the stability of the state'.

The idea of the Boundary Commission had contributed greatly to the divisions which bedevilled Northern Ireland from the start. The Unionists saw it as a threat to their dominance, and their fear of what it would decide meant they kept up their guard against the Nationalist population, avoiding any concessions. Nationalists saw the promise of the Commission as a reason to resist the new state, because they could hope that it would not last long. It was deliberately left vague whether the Boundary Commission was to reorganise the border from scratch, or just to simplify anomalies. However, the Irish had been given the distinct impression that the wishes of the local inhabitants would decide the line of the border.

The Commission sat for a year, touring border areas and examining written submissions. Evidence on behalf of Catholics in the North was received and collated by the Free State's North-East Boundary Bureau. A newspaper leak in November 1925 finally revealed that almost no changes were to be made to the existing border, apart from a small section in County Donegal which was to become part of Northern Ireland. As Fisher wrote to Sir Edward Carson, the retired Unionist leader, '...I am well satisfied with the result which will not shift a stone or tile of your enduring work for Ulster...No centre of even secondary importance goes over, and with Derry, Strabane, Enniskillen, Newtownbutler, Keady and Newry in safe keeping your handiwork will survive'.

MacNeill resigned from the Commission, but too late to prevent himself being deeply discredited. He had interpreted his first loyalty as being to the Commission, rather than to his government, and he had not kept his colleagues informed of events because the Commission insisted on secrecy. In fact, he was probably the only Commission member to fulfil the secrecy requirement completely. In hindsight, the Irish side could have insisted on local plebiscites in the border areas and the North might not have objected, because the loss of some Nationalist areas would probably not have damaged it economically. It never in fact had any economic viability (Westminster controlled 88% of its revenue, and 60% of its expenditure), and a smaller, more homogenous unit would have been easier to run.

The findings of the Commission were never officially published, and the Free State preferred to strike a deal with the British instead. The Boundary Commission was to be revoked, and in exchange the financial obligations of the Free State to Britain under the Treaty were also revoked.

> **Peadar O'Donnell, in Griffith and O'Grady (eds),** *Curious Journey*
> When the news of the Treaty came in December, I felt that was what
> some of us had expected; that the middle-class was getting all they
> wanted, namely the transfer of patronage from Dublin Castle to an
> Irish Parliament. The mere control of patronage did not seem to me
> a sufficient reason for the struggle we had been through...We had
> a pretty barren mind socially; many on the Republican side were
> against change. Had we won, I would agree that the end results
> might not have been much different from what one sees today...

Northern Nationalists felt they had been sold down the river.
They would now have to make the best of their situation,
and Nationalist MPs did begin to enter the Stormont
parliament.

Assessment

What was the point of the Civil War? Hundreds dead and
injured, families split for generations, whole areas of the
country disaffected from the native government, increased
emigration, economic stagnation, severe infrastructural
damage, a legacy of bitterness – and for what? Seventy years
or more after the events described in this book, it is hard to
see it as any more than an enormous waste of lives, resources
and energy that could have been better spent in building a
new state out of a battered ex-colony which was finally
allowed some responsibility for its own affairs, and was
anxious to prove that it could cope.

The ideal of the Republic was no doubt a noble one, but
even reading the Treaty debates, before the war began, it is
obvious that reality was lost sight of at an early stage. The
signatories of the Treaty were not repudiating a living, real
Republic; they were salvaging the best that could be
achieved, with their backs to the wall. Beaslaí put it well
during the debates: 'One would think...that we were solemnly asked to choose between an independent Republic
and an associated Free State. What we are asked is to choose

between this Treaty on the one hand, and, on the other hand, bloodshed, political and social chaos, and the frustration of all our hopes of a national regeneration.'

The Free State government, frustrated by the constant delays and costs of a military campaign, and trying desperately to build what the majority of the population wanted, reacted fiercely to its attackers, and there was no letting bygones be bygones after the fight either. Hundreds of Republican sympathisers lost their jobs, or were unable to find employment; anyone employed in local government or the civil service had to pledge allegiance to the Free State. Large numbers emigrated. The Free State had no National Debt when it was established, but ended the Civil War facing enormous costs, with few resources. As for the basic reason for which the war was fought, Ireland was quite simply declared a Republic in 1949, by Taoiseach John A. Costello, and left the Commonwealth.

The long-standing legacy of bitterness left by Ireland's Civil War has sometimes been attributed to the small size of the population, which would be deeply affected by the numbers of casualties. However Finland, with roughly the same population, suffered a vicious civil war in 1918, which left a total of 25,000 dead, yet former enemies served in government together in 1937. The ghost of Ireland's Civil War was continually invoked in later years, and the bones rattled, largely in order to emphasise the differing roots of the two largest political parties, Fianna Fáil and Fine Gael (successor to Cumann na nGaedheal). Noel Browne gives a vivid description of this: '...As a young

De Valera arrives with members of his new party, Fianna Fáil, to enter the Dáil, 11 August 1927 (Cashman Collection RTE)

Séan Lemass being chaired by supporters after his election to the Dáil in August 1923 – later he would be responsible for the creation of a new Ireland in which the Civil War would become an episode of history (Cashman Collection RTE)

politician in Leinster House [1948], I recall my shock at the white-hot hate with which that terrible episode had marked their lives. The trigger words were "77", "Ballyseedy", "Dick and Joe" and above all "the Treaty" and "damn good bargain". The raised tiers of the Dáil chamber would become filled with shouting, gesticulating, clamouring, suddenly angry men'.

Among other long-lasting results of the Civil War, it has been suggested, was the minor position of women in the political life of the new state. Women TDs had been among the most vehement opponents of the Treaty, and were seen as driving men out to fight. A view developed that politics fostered 'unwomanly' qualities, and women should be discouraged from involving themselves politically. The Republican abstention policy deprived the Dáil of all women TDs except one; for years, Mrs Collins O'Driscoll was the only female representative in the Dáil, and women are still very much in the minority there. Although women had played a prominent role in early twentieth-century Irish politics, their public influence declined dramatically after the Civil War.

Relations with Northern Ireland had been irreparably damaged. The campaign of destabilisation, coupled with a condescending attitude to the Stormont Parliament (seen as a subordinate parliament, compared to the Free State's independent one), created an atmosphere of profound distrust and dislike. Relations between both parts of Ireland existed in a state of Cold War until the Terence O'Neill-Seán Lemass meetings of the 1960s, when the neighbouring prime ministers finally met. After this contacts began to grow warmer and more frequent.

When I started writing this book, I hoped to be able to concentrate some attention on the civilian side rather than the military, which has been dealt with in detail elsewhere. But the Civil War has always been something 'not talked

The memorial at a lonely mountain site in Glencree where the body of Captain Nöel Lemass (brother of Séan Lemass) was dumped after his murder at the hands of Free State forces: such memorials in rural Ireland are part of the tradition of Republican sacrifice (Photo: David Davison)

about', and it was the 1960s before articles began to appear in historical journals about events during that time. These articles came mainly from the protagonists, the fighters; there is still no reservoir of information about civilians, the real heroes of the war. Just as they were beginning to imagine a future after the War of Independence, free from fear and loss, they found that the goalposts had been moved again. They bore the stresses of life during a war, the difficulties of maintaining a normal life, of running a business, of obtaining basic supplies, of clearing up after yet another raid or ambush, not to mention the horror of sudden death and injury. It is time that these stories were resurrected.

'Nearly forty years I've been here, and I don't mean a thing any more.
Good-bye-ee!'
'The Ghost of the Civil War': a 1962 cartoon from the Lemass era (Dublin
Opinion)

ARTICLES OF AGREEMENT FOR A TREATY BETWEEN GREAT BRITAIN AND IRELAND DECEMBER 6, 1921

1. Ireland shall have the same Constitutional status in the community of Nations known as the British Empire as the Dominion of Canada, the Commonwealth of Australia, the Dominion of New Zealand, and the Union of South Africa, with a Parliament having powers to make laws for the peace, order, and good government of Ireland, and an Executive responsible to that Parliament, and shall be styled and known as the Irish Free State.

2. Subject to the provisions hereinafter set out, the position of the Irish Free State in relation to the Imperial Parliament and Government and otherwise shall be that of the Dominion of Canada, and the law, practice, and Constitutional usage governing the relationship of the Crown or the representative of the Crown and of the Imperial Parliament to the Dominion of Canada shall govern their relationship to the Irish Free State.

3. The representative of the Crown in Ireland shall be appointed in like manner as the Governor-General of Canada, and in accordance with the practice observed in the making of such appointments.

4. The Oath to be taken by members of the Parliament of the Irish Free State shall be in the following form:-

I...do solemnly swear true faith and allegiance to the Constitution of the Irish Free State as by law established, and that I will be faithful to H.M. King George V, his heirs and successors by law, in virtue of the common citizenship of Ireland with Great Britain and her adherence to and membership of the group of nations forming the British Commonwealth of Nations.

5. The Irish Free State shall assume liability for the service of the Public Debt of the United Kingdom as existing at the date hereof and towards the payment of War Pensions as existing at that date in such proportion as may be fair and equitable, having regard to any just claim on the part of Ireland by way of set-off or counter-claim, the amount of such sums being determined in default of agreement by the arbitration of one or more independent persons being citizens of the British Empire.

6. Until an arrangement has been made between the British and Irish Governments whereby the Irish Free State undertakes her own coastal defence, the defence by sea of Great Britain and Ireland shall be undertaken by His Majesty's Imperial Forces, but this shall not prevent the construction or maintenance by the Government of the Irish Free State of such vessels as are necessary for the protection of the Revenue or the Fisheries. The foregoing provisions of this Article shall be reviewed at a conference of Representatives of the British and Irish Governments, to be held at the expiration of five years from the date hereof with a view to the undertaking by Ireland of a share in her own coastal defence.

7. The Government of the Irish Free State shall afford to His Majesty's Imperial Forces

(a) In time of peace such harbour and other facilities as are indicated in the Annex hereto, or such other facilities as may from time to time be agreed between the British Government and the Government of the Irish Free State; and

(b) In time of war or of strained relations with a Foreign Power such harbour and other facilities as the British Government may require for the purposes of such defence as aforesaid.

8. With a view to securing the observance of the principle of international limitation of armaments, if the Government of the Irish Free State establishes and maintains a military defence force, the establishments thereof shall not exceed in size such proportion of the military establishments maintained in Great Britain as that which the population of Ireland bears to the population of Great Britain.

9. The ports of Great Britain and the Irish Free State shall be freely open to the ships of the other country on payment of the customary port and other duties.

10. The Government of the Irish Free State agrees to pay fair compensation on terms not less favourable than those accorded by the Act of 1920 to judges, officials, members of Police Forces, and other Public Servants who are discharged by it or who retire in consequence of the change of government effected in pursuance hereof. Provided that this agreement shall not apply to members of the Auxiliary Police Force or to persons recruited in Great Britain for the Royal Irish Constabulary during the two years next preceding the date hereof. The British Government

will assume responsibility for such compensation or pensions as may be payable to any of these excepted persons.

11. Until the expiration of one month from the passing of the Act of Parliament for 'the ratification of this instrument, the powers of the Parliament and the Government of the Irish Free State shall not be exercisable as respects Northern Ireland, and the provisions of the Government of Ireland Act, 1920, shall, so far as they relate to Northern Ireland, remain in full force and effect, and no election shall be held for the return of members to serve in the Parliament of the Irish Free State for constituencies in Northern Ireland, unless a resolution is passed by both Houses of Parliament of Northern Ireland in favour of holding of such elections before the end of the said month.

12. If, before the expiration of the said month, an address is presented to His Majesty by both Houses of Parliament of Northern Ireland to that effect, the powers of the Parliament and the Government of the Irish Free State shall no longer extend to Northern Ireland, and the provisions of the Government of Ireland Act, 1920 (including those relating to the Council of Ireland) shall so far as they relate to Northern Ireland continue to be of full force and effect, and this instrument shall have effect subject to the necessary modifications.

Provided that if such an address is so presented a Commission consisting of three persons, one to be appointed by the Government of the Irish Free State, one to be appointed by the Government of Northern Ireland, and one who shall be Chairman to be appointed by the British Government shall determine in accordance with the wishes of the inhabitants, so far as may be compatible with economic and geographic conditions, the boundaries between Northern Ireland and the rest of Ireland, and for the purposes of the Government of Ireland Act, 1920, and of this instrument, the boundary of Northern Ireland shall be such as may be determined by such Commission.

13. For the purpose of the last foregoing article, the powers of the Parliament of Southern Ireland under the Government of Ireland Act, 1920, to elect members of the Council of Ireland shall after the Parliament of the Irish Free State is constituted be exercised by that Parliament.

14. After the expiration of the said month, if no such address as is mentioned in Article 12 hereof is presented, the Parliament

and Government of Northern Ireland shall continue to exercise as respects Northern Ireland the powers conferred on them by the Government of Ireland Act, 1920, but the Parliament and Government of the Irish Free State shall in Northern Ireland have in relation to matters in respect of which the Parliament of Northern Ireland has not power to make laws under that Act (including matters which under the said Act are within the jurisdiction of the Council of Ireland) the same powers as in the rest of Ireland, subject to such other provisions as may be agreed in manner hereinafter appearing.

15. At any time after the date hereof the Government of Northern Ireland and the provisional Government of Southern Ireland hereinafter constituted may meet for the purpose of discussing the provisions subject to which the last foregoing article is to operate in the event of no such address as is therein mentioned being presented and those provisions may include:-

(a) Safeguards with regard to patronage in Northern Ireland;

(b) Safeguards with regard to the collection of revenue in Northern Ireland;

(c) Safeguards with regard to import and export duties affecting the trade or industry of Northern Ireland;

(d) Safeguards for minorities in Northern Ireland;

(e) The settlement of the financial relations between Northern Ireland and the Irish Free State;

(f) The establishment and powers of a local militia in Northern Ireland and the relation of the Defence Forces of the Irish Free State and of Northern Ireland respectively,

and if at any such meeting provisions are agreed to, the same shall have effect as if they were included amongst the provisions subject to which the powers of the Parliament and the Government of the Irish Free State are to be exercisable in Northern Ireland under article 14 hereof.

16. Neither the Parliament of the Irish Free State nor the Parliament of Northern Ireland shall make any law so as either directly or indirectly to endow any religion or prohibit or restrict the free exercise thereof or give any preference or impose any disability on account of the religious belief or religious status or affect prejudicially the right of any child to attend a school receiving public money without attending the religious instruction at the school or make any discrimination as respects State

aid between schools under the management of different religious denominations or divert from any religious denomination or any educational institution any of its property except for public utility purposes and on payment of compensation.

17. By way of provisional arrangement for the administration of Southern Ireland during the interval which must elapse between the date hereof and the constitution of a Parliament and Government of the Irish Free State in accordance therewith, steps shall be taken forthwith for summoning a meeting of members of Parliament elected for constituencies in Southern Ireland since the passing of the Government of Ireland Act, 1920, and for constituting a provisional Government, and the British Government shall take the steps necessary to transfer to such Provisional Government the powers and machinery requisite for the discharge of its duties provided that every member of such provisional Government shall have signified in writing his or her acceptance of this instrument. But this arrangement shall not continue in force beyond the expiration of twelve months from the date hereof.

18. This instrument shall be submitted forthwith by his Majesty's Government for the approval of Parliament and by the Irish signatories to a meeting summoned for the purpose of the members elected to sit in the House of Commons of Southern Ireland and if approved shall be ratified by the necessary legislation.

Signed

On behalf of the British Delegation:-

D. LLOYD GEORGE.
AUSTEN CHAMBERLAIN.
BIRKENHEAD.
WINSTON S. CHURCHILL.
L.WORTHINGTON EVANS.
HAMAR GREENWOOD.
GORDON HEWART.

On behalf of the Irish Delegation:

ART Ó GRIOBHTHA.
MICHEAL O COILEAIN.
RIOBARD BARTÚN.
E.S. Ó DUGAIN.
SEORSA GABHAIN
UI DHUBHTHAIGH.

6th December, 1921.

QUOTES FROM TREATY DEBATES
(Private Sessions)

COMMANDANT SEAN MCKEON: We are told by the Minister of Defence that the army is in a much stronger position, indefinitely stronger now than it was before the Truce – well it may. It may be stronger in some points. in point of members it is a bit stronger – in training it is a bit stronger ... I know perfectly well I have charge of four thousand men. I do not here hesitate to say that number. But of that four thousand I have a rifle for every fifty. Now that is the position as far as I am concerned and I may add that there is about as much ammunition as would last them about fifty minutes for that one rifle. Now people talk lightly of when we are going to war. I hold they do not know a damn thing about it (hear, hear)....

***

MR. ETCHINGHAM: ...No I tell you here that the only true shade of Republicanism is the one who stands true to the separatist principles. I do not wish to speak of personal matters but I may say that my mother, who is 84 years old, when the soldiers came to blow up her home and my home and the home of her sister, what did she say to them? 'You may level every house in it but you won't kill the country', and I can't go back to her and say that I voted for this wretched thing ... I will also speak plainly to the men here. Thanks be to God it is not necessary for the women, for the women in the Dáil will show they are the best men in it. I am told Ireland was always fond of kings. They were never Republican. You want a king, do you? If you want a king make a king of a gander or a puckaun but in God's name let it be an Irish gander or a puckaun. Why go to England for a gander?

MR. PIARAS BEASLAI: ...This is a Treaty now at the cannon's mouth in guerilla warfare from a power against whom we could never expect a military decision in our favour. This power is to leave the country bag and baggage, to withdraw from all her strong fortified positions and to leave the country in possession of the Irish army, the very thing we have been fighting for and now achieve for the first time in 750 years.

MR. C. BRUGHA: Will you give me two or three minutes? I will ask the indulgence of this body to listen to what I have to say without interruption. I can forgive the five men who have landed us into the present position because I realised before ever they went there – mind you I was against their ever going to England, I said this conference should be held in a neutral country – I realised before ever they went there the terrible influence that would be brought to bear upon them. We have got proof of that.

MR. GAVAN DUFFY: Where is it?

MR. ML. COLLINS: On a point of order, Mr. Chairman please, I must insist on this. It is for us to explain our mental condition in London, not for somebody else (Hear hear)....There is a lot of talk about the question of whether the delegates exceeded their instructions. These delegates were in a very difficult position. There is a tide in the affairs of nations as in the affairs of men which when taken at flood time often results in a great advantage to the country.

A MEMBER: It takes you out to sea sometimes.

***

MR. O'SULLIVAN: We have never heard of an oath of allegiance to individuals in this country. We always found these things very hard to swallow. I was enquiring from some friends what exactly this oath meant. You will be told if it means anything from a hundred other things, first it is an oath of allegiance to Ireland. When the Parliament of the new Government of Ireland is set up it will draw up its own constitution to which you are loyal and once said you will be faithful to the king because he is one of the contracting parties. Suppose this person said when a man gets married he promises to be faithful to his wife which is a very different thing from owning allegiance to her (A voice, 'Wait until you get married'). Other Deputies insist on telling me their domestic troubles. He explained to me according to English law if one party to the contract is unfaithful that a contract is dissolved. I do not know whether we are bound down in this Assembly to swear that at no future date will we divorce King George but I do know that we certainly cannot swear for the next generation or any other....

***

MR. NICHOLLS: ...When I find the combined brains of the members of the delegation – Arthur Griffith, Michael Collins, Eamonn Duggan, Robert Barton and Gavan Duffy – when we find their combined brains bringing us home this, when I find these combined brains coupled with the spirit of men like Commdt. McKeon, Gearoid O'Sullivan and the numerous survivors of Easter Week that are here, I must certainly say it seems good enough for me in any case. We are appealed to in the name of the dead. I would like to lay great stress on the fact that it is only by the merest coincidence that a great number of members that are here present are alive. They fought for the same principle as the men who died and anyone who would suggest to me that they would be false, well I must say that I cannot understand that person's mind....

***

MR. P. BRENNAN: ...She (Miss MacSwiney) stated that you will find no woman who has suffered who would think of accepting this Treaty or something similar. Well, the wife of Christy McCarthy who was killed in action a few weeks before the Truce spoke to me and asked me for God's sake to vote for the Treaty and not plunge the country into war again. She stated also that the people would be behind us in the new fight but they would not be behind with the same heart as they showed in the last fight....

DR. WHITE: ...The Oath, I suggest, in this Treaty is the oath of the Free State of Ireland. So far as that is concerned I am very easy in my mind. The people of Ireland are taking that Oath under duress and I, as a representative, have consulted as many as I could of my people before I came to Dublin and they were in favour of my voting for this Treaty. I will do as they suggest.... Now this Treaty has been called a shadow. I respectfully submit that it contains 90 per cent of the substance and I further say that the shadow of England has disappeared practically to the minimum and I for one as a plain Irishman fail to see what more we could do from an economic point of view and for the development of the country under a Republic than we could do under this measure of the Treaty...

***

MR. LYNCH: I understand you to say that the only thing within the power of the Dáil is to recommend it to the country. I also wanted to know, if it was in the power of the Dáil to prevent a split that those who stand for the Treaty should come over. Now I hold it is not the people who stand for the Treaty who are going to be responsible for the split. I hold it is the people who go out from this Assembly to the country who will cause a split. Now I will give my reasons briefly for standing for the Treaty. I stand for it inasmuch as it gives this country an army in the first instance. I am not a great soldier and I am not going to boast about my heroism. I cannot boast about any heroism because when the real war came on I was unanimously [*sic*] captured and I spent my time in jail nice and safe when other men were fighting. But I did my best. I stand for the Treaty because it gives this country control over education. It gives it an opportunity of building up the Gaelic state as was referred to by somebody yesterday. It gives the country control over its own finances; something that we have been hearing a lot about for many years past as the be-all and the end-all of Irish aspirations. It gets finally the British army out of Ireland and even though my friend Deputy Etchingham says that it only exchanges the khaki man for the marines we have got both the marines and the khaki men here now. (Deputy: And the Black and Tans). And this document put up by the President provides for the marines just as the Treaty does....This Treaty we have been told over and over in the House is a compromise. It is a compromise and so is that of the President. The difference is just a matter of degree. This compromise Document No. 2 leads you nowhere but into war. The other compromise delivers some kind of goods....

***

MRS. MARGARET PEARSE: ...Since 1916, with the exception of the visits of the Black and Tans I had comfortable nights' rest, but if I signed that Treaty or accepted it I assure you I would not have any night's rest, for I would be haunted by the ghosts of my sons. I hope in God that I will see that while I see here tonight several men who are wrong that they will come right and will do what Padraig Pearse would have done ... do they think that the man who spoke as he did at O'Donovan Rossa's grave would accept that Treaty? No, nor neither would his brother or his mother. I have several letters from people who sent me here reminding me of my duty. There was no necessity to remind me of it. They should know me. They pointed out to me how they elected me and what they elected me for – to do my duty, and I mean to.

BIOGRAPHICAL NOTES

Aiken, Frank (1898-1983) Commdt. 4th Northern Division IRA; Chief of Staff, anti-Treaty forces, 1923; founder member of Fianna Fáil 1926; held five government Ministries; Tanaiste 1965-9.

Barry, Tom (1897-1980) Fought in British Army, World War I; commanded West Cork IRA unit, War of Independence; anti-Treaty during Civil War; ceased IRA activity 1940.

Barton, Robert (1881-1975) Cousin of Erskine Childers; fought in British Army, World War I; Sinn Féin TD, first Minister for Agriculture 1919-21; member of Treaty delegation; took anti-Treaty side; retired from politics after Civil War.

Beaslaí, Piaras (1881-1965) Worked with Michael Collins during War of Independence; Sinn Féin TD; Major-General in Free State Army; retired 1924, to work for Irish language movement.

Blythe, Ernest (1889-1975) Irish Volunteer organiser; Sinn Féin TD; held four government Ministries; Vice-President, Executive Council of Irish Free State, 1923-32; Director of Abbey Theatre, 1939-67.

Boland, Harry (1887-1922) IRB member, imprisoned after 1916 Rising; secretary of Sinn Féin and TD; accompanied Eamon de Valera on United States trip, 1919-21; rejected Treaty; shot while resisting arrest.

Breen, Dan (1894-1969) Active with Third Tipperary Brigade, IRA, during War of Independence; Sinn Féin TD; imprisoned during Civil War; first Republican to take Oath of Allegiance, April 1927.

Brennan, Michael (1896-1986) Commander, East Clare Brigade, IRA, during War of Independence; Commandant, 1st Western Division, Free State Army; Chief of Staff, 1931-40.

Brugha, Cathal (1874-1922) Second-in-command at South Dublin Union garrison during 1916 Rising, severely injured; Sinn Féin TD; Minister for National Defence; occupied Four Courts at start of Civil War; shot during fighting.

Childers, Erskine (1870-1922) Served in British Army during Boer War; used his yacht *Asgard* in gun-running for Irish Volunteers, 1914; in Royal Navy air force, 1916, awarded DSO; Sinn Féin TD, Director of Publicity; member of Treaty delegation; Director of Publicity, anti-Treaty forces; executed.

Clarke, Kathleen (1878-1972) Wife of Tom Clarke, IRB leader, and sister to Commdt Ned Daly, Irish Volunteers, both executed after 1916 Rising; Sinn Féin TD; Senator 1937; first woman Lord Mayor of Dublin, 1939.

Collins, Michael (1890-1922) IRB member, fought in GPO during 1916 Rising; after imprisonment, Secretary of Irish National Aid

Fund; controlled IRA intelligence system, War of Independence; Minister for Home Affairs, First Dáil, later Minister for Finance; member of Treaty delegation; Chairman of Provisional Government; Commander-in-Chief, Free State Army; shot in ambush.

Comerford, Maire (1893-1989) Joined Sinn Féin after 1916 Rising; member Cumann na mBan; in Four Courts during Civil War; imprisoned; 27 days hunger-strike; life-long Sinn Féin member.

Cosgrave, William T. (1880-1965) Fought in GPO during 1916 Rising; treasurer, Sinn Féin; Minister for Local Government, First Dáil; President of Second Dáil, 1922; Chairman of Provisional Government; founded Cumann na nGaedheal, 1923; President Executive Council 1923-32; retired 1944.

Craig, Sir James (1st Viscount Craigavon) (1871-1940) Northern Ireland Unionist MP, 1906-18; fought in British Army, World War I; first Prime Minister, Northern Ireland, 1921-40.

de Valera, Eamon (1882-1975) Commandant, 3rd Brigade Irish Volunteers, during 1916 Rising; Sinn Féin TD; President Sinn Féin 1917-26; President First Dáil, 1919; Involved in Truce talks; rejected Treaty; accepted defeat, 1923; founded Fianna Fáil 1926, entered Dail 1927; Taoiseach 1937-48, 1951-4, 1957-9; President, Irish Republic, 1959-73.

Duffy, George Gavan (1882-1951) Sinn Féin TD; member of Treaty delegation; Minister for Foreign Affairs, Second Dáil; resigned 1922; President of High Court, 1946.

Duggan, E.J. (1874-1936) Fought in GPO during 1916 Rising; Director of Intelligence, Irish Volunteers; Sinn Féin TD; member of Treaty delegation; held three government Ministries; elected to Senate, 1933.

FitzGerald, Desmond (1889-1947) Fought in GPO during 1916 Rising; Sinn Féin TD; Director of Propaganda, War of Independence; held three government Ministries; Senator, 1938-47.

Griffith, Arthur (1871-1922) Member of IRB till 1910; developed Sinn Féin policy of economic self-sufficiency; Irish Volunteer, but no military part in 1916 Rising; Acting President of First Dáil during de Valera's US tour 1919-21; headed Treaty delegation; defeated de Valera for Presidency.

Hogan, Patrick J. (1891-1936) Sinn Féin TD; Minister for Agriculture 1922-32; lost seat in 1932, became Senator.

Johnson, Thomas (1872-1963) Founder member of Irish Labour Party, 1912; co-author of Democratic Programme adopted by First Dáil; accused of supporting Treaty, stayed neutral; leader of Labour Party and official Dáil opposition until 1927, when lost seat; Senator until 1936; founder member of Labour Court, 1946.

Lemass, Sean (1900-71) Fought in GPO during 1916 Rising; fought in War of Independence; member of Four Courts garrison; Sinn Féin TD; Fianna Fáil Minister for Industry and Commerce 1932-48 (with brief break), 1951-54, 1957-9; Tanaiste 1945; Taoiseach 1959-66.

Lynch, Liam (1890-1923) Commander, Cork No. 2 Brigade IRA, War of Independence; member of Supreme Council, IRB; Chief-of-Staff, anti-Treaty IRA, 1922; commander, 1st Southern Division, anti-Treaty IRA; 30.11.22, issued 'Orders of Frightfulness', outlining categories of people to be shot on sight, such as TDs; shot by Free State forces during skirmish.

MacBride, Maud Gonne (1866-1953) Led agitations over land system, amnesty for IRB prisoners, support for Boers; founded Inghinidhe na hEireann (Daughters of Erin), republican/suffragette group, 1900; married to Major John MacBride, who was executed after 1916 Rising; 20 days' hunger- strike while imprisoned during Civil War; founded Women's Prisoners Defence League; mother of *Sean MacBride*, anti-Treaty IRA, founder of Clann na Poblachta party (1946).

MacEoin, Sean (1894-1973) IRA commander during War of Independence, known as 'Blacksmith of Ballinalee' (his home village) after defeat of Black and Tans attack; GOC Western Command, Free State Army; Chief of Staff 1923; Sinn Féin TD; two Ministries in Inter-Party Governments, 1948-51, 1954-7; retired 1965.

McGrath, Joseph (1888-1966) Fought in 1916 Rising; Sinn Féin TD; Minister for Labour, Second Dáil; Minister for Industry and Commerce 1922-24; resigned after Army Mutiny; founder of Irish Hospitals Sweepstakes.

MacNeill, Eoin (1867-1945) Professor of Early & Mediaeval Irish History, University College Dublin, 1908; Chief-of-Staff, Irish Volunteers; attempted to postpone 1916 Rising; Sinn Féin TD, three Ministries in First Dáil and Provisional Government; Free State representative on Boundary Commission, 1924-5; resigned after results leaked.

MacSwiney, Mary (1872-1942) Sister of Terence MacSwiney, who died after 72 days' hunger-strike in Brixton Prison; established St Ita's school, 1916; Sinn Féin TD; ran republican HQ, Cork, during Civil War; never recognised legitimacy of Free State.

Markievicz, Constance (1868-1927) Founded Irish youth organisation, Fianna Eireann, 1909; member Inghinidhe na hEireann; officer, Irish Citizen Army; fought in Stephen's Green, 1916 Rising; first woman elected to British House of Commons, 1918 (did not take seat); Minister for Labour, First Dáil, 1919-21; President of anti-Treaty Cumann na mBan.

Mellows, Liam (1892-1922) IRB member, fought in 1916 Rising; acted as advance agent for de Valera's US tour 1919-21; Director of Purchases, IRA, War of Independence; Sinn Féin TD; member of Four Courts garrison; executed.

Mulcahy, Richard (1886-1971) Fought at Ashbourne, 1916 Rising; Chief-of-Staff, Irish Volunteers, 1917; Sinn Féin TD; Minister for Defence, Provisional Government; resigned after Army Mutiny, 1924; founder-member of Fine Gael, 1933; three Ministries in Inter-Party governments; retired 1959.

O'Connell, J.J. ('Ginger') (1887-1944) Commander of Irish Volunteers, Cork, 1916 Rising; Assistant Chief-of-Staff, IRA, War of Independence; his kidnapping precipitated attack on Four Courts; held various posts in Free State army after Civil War.

O'Connor, Rory (1883-1922) IRB member, fought in 1916 Rising; Director of Engineering, IRA, War of Independence; chairman, Military Council, anti-Treaty IRA; member of Four Courts garrison, captured; executed.

O'Duffy, Eoin (1892-1944) Member of HQ staff, IRA, War of Independence; Sinn Féin TD; Assistant Chief-of-Staff, Free State Army, GOC South-Western Command; first commander, Garda Síochána (police force), 1922; dismissed by de Valera, 1933; commander, National Guard ('Blueshirts'), declared illegal 1933; founder-member, Fine Gael; led 600 Irish Franco supporters to Spanish Civil War, 1936-7; Fascist sympathiser during World War II.

O'Higgins, Kevin (1892-1927) Member Irish Volunteers; Sinn Féin TD; Minister for Home Affairs 1922-7; member of drafting committee, 1922 Constitution; represented Free State at League of Nations; assassinated.

O'Malley, Ernie (1898-1957) Fought in 1916 Rising; organiser for Michael Collins, War of Independence; commander, 2nd Southern Division IRA; member of Four Courts garrison; O/C Northern and Eastern anti-Treaty IRA; imprisoned 1922-4; hunger-strike, 41 days; Sinn Féin TD; settled in Mexico and USA, 1927-35; elected to Irish Academy of Letters, 1947, for autobiographies and other writings.

Stack, Austin (1880-1929) Commandant, Irish Volunteers, 1916 Rising; Sinn Féin TD; Minister for Home Affairs, First Dáil; supported anti-Treaty IRA; imprisoned, hunger-strike.

Traynor, Oscar (1886-1963) Fought in 1916 Rising; O/C Dublin Brigade, IRA, War of Independence; ordered Four Courts garrison to surrender; founder-member, Fianna Fáil, held three Ministries.

Wilson, Sir Henry (1864-1922) Served in British Army, Boer War; Assistant Chief of General Staff, France, World War I; Unionist MP for County Down; security adviser to Sir James Craig; assassinated.

BIBLIOGRAPHY

ANGLO-IRISH TREATY

Curran, J.M. 'Lloyd George and the Irish Settlement 1921-22' (*Eire-Ireland* Vol VII, 1972)

de Burca, P. and Boyle, John F. *Free State or Republic? Pen Pictures of the Historic Treaty Session of Dáil Eireann* (Talbot Press, 1922)

Dwyer, T. Ryle *Michael Collins and the Treaty* (Mercier, 1981)

Gallagher, Frank *The Anglo-Irish Treaty* (Hutchinson, 1965)

Gallagher, Michael 'The Pact General Election of 1922' (*Irish Historical Studies* Vol XXI , 1979)

Hawkings, F.M.A. 'Defence and the Role of Erskine Childers in the Treaty Negotiations of 1921' (*Irish Historical Studies* Vol. XXII, 1981)

Lawlor, S.M.' Ireland from Truce to Treaty - War or Peace? July to October 1921' (*Irish Historical Studies* Vol. XXII, 1980)

McColgan, John 'Implementing the 1921 Treaty: Lionel Curtis and constitutional procedure' (*Irish Historical Studies* XX, 1977)

Pakenham, Frank *Peace by Ordeal* (Chapman, 1962)

Towey, Thomas 'The Reaction of the British Government to the 1922 Collins-de Valera Pact' (*Irish Historical Studies* Vol. XXII, 1980)

BIOGRAPHY/MEMOIR

Andrews, C.S. *Dublin Made Me* (Mercier Press, 1979)

Beaslai, Piaras *Michael Collins and the Making of a New Ireland* (Dublin, 1926)

Brennan, Robert *Allegiance* (Browne & Nolan, 1950)

Buckley, Margaret *The Jangle of the Keys* (Duffy & Co, Dublin, 1938)

Clarke, Kathleen *Revolutionary Woman* (O'Brien Press, 1991)

Coogan, Tim Pat *De Valera - Long Fellow, Long Shadow* (London, 1993)

Coxhead, Elizabeth *Daughters of Erin* (London, 1965)

Deasy, Liam *Brother against Brother* (Mercier Press, 1982)

Donnelly, Brian (ed) 'The National Army Enters Cork August 1992: A Diary Account by Mr Frank Brewitt' (*Irish Archives*, Autumn 1994)

Dwyer, T. Ryle *De Valera: The Man & The Myths* (Poolbeg Press, 1991)

Edwards, O. Dudley *Eamon de Valera* (GPC Press, 1987)

English, R. and O'Malley, C. *Prisoners: The Civil War Letters of Ernie O'Malley* (Poolbeg Press, 1991)

Farrell, Brian *Sean Lemass* (Gill and Macmillan, 1983)

Fingall, Elizabeth Countess of *Seventy Years Young* (1937, reprinted Lilliput Press, 1991)

Forester, Margery *Michael Collins - The Lost Leader* (1971)

Greaves, T.D. *Liam Mellows and the Irish Revolution* (London, 1971)

Griffiths, K. and O'Grady, T. E. *Curious Journey* (Hutchinson, 1982)

Hammond, Bill *Soldier of the Rearguard* (Fermoy, 1977)

Irish Times *Eamon de Valera 1882-1975* (Irish Times, 1976)

Irwin, Wilmot *Betrayal in Ireland* (Northern Whig, 1968)

Lee, J. and O Tuathaigh, G. *The Age of de Valera* (Ward River, 1982)

Longford, Earl of and O'Neill, T.P. *Eamon de Valera* (Gill and Macmillan, 1970)

MacEoin, Uinseann (ed) *Survivors* (Argenta, 1980)

Neeson, Eoin *The Life and Death of Michael Collins* (Mercier Press, 1968)

Nevinson, Henry W. *Last Changes, Last Chances* (London, 1928)

Norman, Diana *Terrible Beauty: A Life of Constance Markievicz* (1987)

O Broin, Leon *In Great Haste: Letters of Michael Collins and Kitty Kiernan* (1983)

O'Connor, Frank *An Only Child* (Macmillan, 1958)

The Big Fellow (Nelson, 1937)

O'Connor, Seamus *Tomorrow was Another Day* (Anvil Books, 1970)

O'Donnell, Jim 'Recollections based on

the diary of an Irish Volunteer' (*Cathair na Mart* 10,1, 1990; 11, 1991)

O'Donnell, Peadar *There Will Be Another Day* (Dolmen Press, 1963)

O'Malley, Ernie *The Singing Flame* (Anvil Books, 1978)

O'Rahilly, Aodogan 'The Civil War: A teenager's recollections 70 years on' (*Tipperary Historical Journal*, 1991)

Ryan, Lt-Col Thomas 'One Man's Flying Column' (*Tipperary Historical Journal*, 1991)

Taylor, Rex *Michael Collins* (Hutchinson, 1958)

Tierney, Michael *Eoin MacNeill: Scholar and Man of Action, 1867-1945* (Oxford University Press, 1980)

Valiulis, Maryann G. *Portrait of a Revolutionary: General Richard Mulcahy* (Irish Academic Press, 1992)

Van Voris, Jacqueline *Constance de Markievicz: In the Cause of Ireland* (Massachusetts, 1967)

Ward, Margaret *Maud Gonne* (Pandora, 1990)

In Their Own Voice: Women and Irish Nationalism (Attic Press, 1995)

White, T. de Vere *Kevin O'Higgins* (Methuen, 1967)

CIVIL WAR

Akenson, D. H. and Fallin, J. F. ' The Irish Civil War and the drafting of the Free State Constitution' (*Eire-Ireland* Vol V, 1970)

Conway, An t-Athair Colmcille 'The Third Tipperary Brigade' (1921-1923) (*Tipperary Historical Journal*, 1990, 9-26; 1991 35-49; 1992 23-30)

Cunningham, John B. 'The Struggle for the Belleek-Pettigo Salient, 1922' (*Donegal Annual* 34,1982)

Curran, J.M. *The Birth of the Irish Free State 1921-23* (Alabama, 1980)

Harrington, Niall *The Kerry Landing, August 1922* (Anvil Books, 1992)

Hart, Peter M. 'Michael Collins and the assassination of Sir Henry Wilson' (*Irish Historical Studies* XXVIII, 1992)

Hopkinson, Michael *Green Against Green: The Irish Civil War* (Gill and Macmillan 1988)

MacArdle, Dorothy *Tragedies of Kerry 1922-1923* (Dublin, 1924)

Neeson, Eoin *The Civil War in Ireland 1921-23* (Mercier Press, 1966)

O'Beirne Ranelagh, John 'The IRB from the Treaty to 1924' (*Irish Historical Studies* XX, 1976)

Ryan, Meda *The Day Michael Collins Was Shot* (Poolbeg Press, 1989)

Sharkey, Neil The Third Tipperary Brigade: A Photographic Record (*Tipperary Historical Journal* 1994 9-25)

Valiulis, Maryann G. 'The Man They Could Never Forgive : de Valera & the Civil War' in O'Carroll & Murphy, *De Valera & His Times* (1983)

Younger, Calton *Ireland's Civil War* (London, 1968)

DRAMA/LITERATURE

Costello, Peter *The Heart Grown Brutal: The Irish Revolution in Literature (1891-1939)* (Gill and Macmillan, 1977)

O'Casey, Sean *Juno and The Paycock*

O'Connor, Ulick *Executions* (Brandon Books, 1992)

The Treaty (Video, Merlin Films for Thames/RTE, Producer/Director Jonathan Lewis)

NORTHERN IRELAND

Bardon, Jonathan *A History of Ulster* (Blackstaff Press, 1992)

Bowman, John *De Valera and the Ulster Question 1917-1973* (OUP, 1982)

Buckland, Patrick *Irish Unionism Vol 2: Ulster Unionism and the Origins of Northern Ireland 1886-1922* (Gill & Macmillan, 1973)

Gonne, Maud 'The Real Case Against Partition' (*Capuchin Annual* 1943 pp. 320-22)

Hand, G.J. 'MacNeill and the Boundary Commission' in Martin and Byrne (eds), *The Scholar Revolutionary, Eoin MacNeill 1867- 1945* (IUP 1973)

Harkness, David *Northern Ireland Since 1920* (Helicon, 1983)

Hopkinson, Michael 'The Craig-Collins Pacts of 1922: two attempted reforms of the Northern Ireland government' (*Irish Historical Studies* Vol. XXVII, 1990)

Kennedy, Dennis *The Widening Gulf: Northern attitudes to the independent Irish state 1919-49* (Blackstaff Press, 1988)

McColgan, John 'Partition and the Irish Administration 1920-22' (*Administration* Vol. 28, 1980)

Mansergh, Nicholas *The Unresolved Question: The Anglo-Irish Settlement and its Undoing 1912-72* (New Haven and London, 1991)

O'Halloran, Clare *Partition and the Limits of Irish Nationalism* (Gill & Macmillan 1987)

Phoenix, Eamon *Northern Nationalism, 1890-1940* (Ulster Historical Foundation, 1994)

OTHER

Boyce, D.G. (ed) *The Revolution in Ireland, 1879-1923* (Macmillan, 1988)

Brennan, Robert *Allegiance* (Browne & Nolan, 1950)

Browne, Noel *Against the Tide* (Gill and Macmillan, 1986)

Canning, Paul *British Policy Towards Ireland 1921-1941* (Oxford, 1985)

Conlon, Lil *Cumann na mBan and the Women of Ireland 1913-25* (Kilkenny People, 1969)

Cullen, L.M. *Eason & Son, A History* (Eason, 1989)

Fanning, Ronan *Independent Ireland* (Dublin, 1983)

The Irish Department of Finance 1922-58 (1978)

Fitzgerald, William G. (ed) *The Voice of Ireland* (1924)

Fitzpatrick, David (ed) *Revolution? Ireland 1917-1923* (Trinity History Workshop, 1990)

Garvin, Tom *The Evolution of Irish Nationalist Politics* (Gill and Macmillan, 1981)

Harkness, David *The Restless Dominion: The Irish Free State and the British Commonwealth of Nations, 1921-31* (Macmillan, 1969)

Hepburn, A.C. *The Conflict of Nationality in Modern Ireland* (London, 1980)

Hill, R.J. and Marsh, M. (eds) *Modern Irish Democracy* (Irish Academic Press, 1993)

Hoppen, K. Theodore *Ireland Since 1800: Conflict & Conformity* (Longman, 1989)

Jones, Mary *These Obstreperous Lassies: A History of the Irish Women Workers' Union* (1988)

Kee, Robert *The Green Flag* (London, 1972)

Lawlor, Sheila *Britain & Ireland 1914-23* (Gill and Macmillan, 1983)

Lyons, F.S.L. *Ireland Since the Famine* (London, 1971)

MacArdle, Dorothy *The Irish Republic* (Dublin, 1951)

McCarthy, Charles *Trade Unions in Ireland 1894-1960* (Dublin, 1977)

McColgan, John *British Policy and the Irish Administration 1920-22* (Dublin, 1983)

McKillen, Beth 'Irish Feminism and Nationalist Separatism, 1914-1923' (*Eire-Ireland* Vol XVII, 1982)

McRedmond, Louis *Ireland, The Revolutionary Years: Photographs from the Cashman Collection* (Gill and Macmillan, 1992)

McCarthy, P.J. 'The RAF and Ireland 1920-22' (*Irish Sword* XVII, 1989)

Mitchell, Arthur *Revolutionary Government in Ireland: Dáil Eireann 1919-22* (Gill and Macmillan, 1995)

Moody, T.W. (ed) *Nationality and the Pursuit of National Independence* (Appletree, 1978)

O Broin, Leon *Protestant Nationalists in Revolutionary Ireland: The Stopford Connection* (Gill & Macmillan, 1985)

O'Brien, Conor Cruise (ed) *The Shaping of Modern Ireland* (London, 1960)

O'Sullivan, Donal *The Irish Free State and its Senate - a study in contemporary politics* (Faber & Faber, 1940)

Valiulis, Maryann G. *Almost a Rebellion: the Irish army mutiny of 1924* (Tower Books, 1985)

'The army mutiny of 1924 and the assertion of civilian authority in independent Ireland' (*Irish Historical Studies* XXIII, 1983)

Ward, Margaret *Unmanageable Revolutionaries* (Brandon Books, 1983)

Williams, T.D. (ed) *The Irish Struggle, 1916-1926* (London, 1966)

INDEX

THE IRISH FAMINE:
An Illustrated History

Helen Litton

'As a short intellient overview of 1845 – 50,
it will be hard to surpass.' *RTE Guide*
'The best documented study, with first-hand accounts
and up-to-date studies.' *Cork Examiner*
'Highly recommended.' *In Dublin*

This is an account of one of the most significant — and tragic — events in Irish history. The author, Helen Litton, deals with the emotive subject of the Great Famine clearly and succinctly, documenting the causes and their effects. With quotes from first-hand accounts, and relying on the most up-to-date studies, she describes the mixture of ignorance, confusion, inexperience and vested interests that lay behind the 'good *v* evil' image of popular perception.

Here are the people who tried to influence events — politicians like Peel, public servants like Trevelyan, Quaker relief workers, local committees, clergy and landlords — who wrestled with desperate need, and sometimes gave up in despair. Why did millions of starving people seem to accept their fate without rebelling? Why starvation on the very shores of seas and rivers plentifully stocked with fish?

This is a story of individuals such as Denis McKennedy — dying in Cork in 1846 because his Board of Works wages were two weeks late — and of a society in crisis. It should be read by anyone who seeks a fuller understanding of the Irish past.

Helen Litton took her Master of Arts degree in History at University College Dublin. She is a leading Irish reseracher, editor and indexer.

ISBN 0-86327-427-7

Gerald Keegan's FAMINE DIARY
Journey to a New World

Edited by James Mangan

'Heart-rending and powerful.' *Irish Times*
'A compelling account.' *Cork Examiner*

In 1847 Gerald Keegan was newly wed when he left County Sligo with his young bride to travel on a coffin ship to Canada. This is a fictionalised narrative by James Mangan based on this nineteenth century diary.

0-86327-300-9

NO SHOES IN SUMMER
Days to Remember

Editors: Mary Ryan, Sean Browne
& Kevin Gilmour

'There is good journalism, fine storytelling and great social history ....' *Sunday Tribune*

Born between the 1890s and the 1930s, the contributors share memories of nearly three centuries of Irish life: of 1916, the Shadows of War; of villages long gone, the Changing Face of Ireland; of 'crossing the Liffey', of bicycles, of pishogues, of Christmases Past, of Love and Laughter, of Scut the Whip and Spin the Top, of Walking to School and of No Shoes in Summer.

As Eilís Dillon points out in the foreword: a collection of this nature has never before been published in Ireland. It is the first time that an unsanitised, local voice has been given a platform.

0-86327-487-0

PROVERBS AND SAYINGS OF IRELAND

Edited by Seamus Cashman
and Sean Gaffney
Illustrated by Robert Gibbings

'A proverbial bestseller!' *Sunday Press*
'Over 1,000 fascinating, witty, cynical and totally Irish
aphorisms...' *Evening Herald*
'Valuable and entertaining insight into the wisdom and
culture of Ireland.' *The Standard*
0-86327-432-3

FATHERS AND SONS

Compiled by Tom Hyde

What is it about the father-son connection that leaves so much unsaid? Why, for so many men, is it a deep-rooted source of hurt, confusion, dissatisfaction and even bitterness?

In *Fathers and Sons*, more than twenty men express with courage and honesty what they truly feel about their fathers.

The contributors are men from diverse walks of life, and include the writers Joe O'Connor, Hugh Leonard and William Trevor, the poets Brendan Kennelly and Seamus Heaney, Jim and Peter Sheridan, politician Sean Haughey, Garret Fitzgerald, Michael D Higgins and many more. It is a searching, poignant, and ultimately healing read.

0-86327-515-X

FATHER BROWNE'S
AUSTRALIA

E. E. O'Donnell

'a master photographer with an unerring eye.'
London *Independent*
**'the most important documentary historian of this
century.'** *Irish Times*

Next in the acclaimed **Father Browne** series, following on
*Father Browne's Ireland, Father Browne's Dublin, The
Genius of Father Browne,* and *A Life in Pictures.*

Affected by gassing in WWI, Fr. Browne was sent on a
voyage to Australia for health reasons. He spent two years (from
1925 - 1927) taking over 900 photographs and this volume
presents the cream of the collection from the developing cities
to the wild Outback.

0-86327-443-9

FATHER BROWNE'S
CORK

Here are flashing insights on the personalities of Cork men,
women and children; panoramic shots of land and sea, featur-
ing, for example, the Mizen cliffs and Garnish Island; famous Great
Houses and churches; pictorial slices of history, and many instances
of what can only be described as 'curiosities'...

0-86327-489-7

These books are available from all good bookshops or direct from
WOLFHOUND PRESS,
68 Mountjoy Square,
Dublin 1.
Tel: 8740354 Fax: 8720207.